Your Towns and Cities in the

Carlisle in the Great War

Dedication

For Jan, with love

Your Towns and Cities in the Great War

Carlisle in the Great War

David Carter

First published in Great Britain in 2014 by
PEN & SWORD MILITARY
an imprint of
Pen and Sword Books Ltd
47 Church Street
Barnsley
South Yorkshire S70 2AS

ISBN 978 1 78337 613 1

A CIP record for this book is available from the British Library

Printed and bound in England
by CPI Group (UK) Ltd, Croydon, CR0 4YY

Typeset in Times New Roman by Chic Graphics

Pen & Sword Books Ltd incorporates the imprints of
Pen & Sword Archaeology, Atlas, Aviation, Battleground, Discovery,
Family History, History, Maritime, Military, Naval, Politics, Railways,
Select, Social History, Transport, True Crime, and Claymore Press,
Frontline Books, Leo Cooper, Praetorian Press, Remember When,
Seaforth Publishing and Wharncliffe.

For a complete list of Pen and Sword titles please contact
Pen and Sword Books Limited
47 Church Street, Barnsley, South Yorkshire, S70 2AS, England
E-mail: enquiries@pen-and-sword.co.uk
Website: www.pen-and-sword.co.uk

Contents

Acknowledgements

This book could not have been completed without the invaluable support of three of Carlisle's local historians, Denis Perriam, Ashley Kendall and Mike Milbourn, who generously shared information and provided illustrations; Denis also kindly read and commented on a draft of the book. Stephen White at Carlisle City Library willingly answered questions and provided difficult to find sources. Dr Chris Brader at Cumbria archive in Carlisle shared his article on cinema in Carlisle and with his colleagues gave advice and guidance. Andrew Carter of BBC Cumbria collaborated with me to find information. Patrick Brennan's research on the munitonettes football teams was a superb source. Sheila Ruddick and her colleagues at the Devil's Porridge factory museum at Eastriggs clarified obscure points about life in the munitions factory. Sue Light, a member of the *Great War Forum*, provided details about the management of hospitals. I am also grateful to the editor of the *Cumberland News* for permission to use pictures and adverts from the *Carlisle Journal.*

Robin Acland of U3A and Richard Preston shared ideas and information about the county which helped to set my reading into a wider context. John Hughes, a friend and neighbour, revealed that his grandparents met at Gretna and provided previously unpublished pictures and material.

As ever my long-suffering wife, Jan, gave unstinting support and acted as a sounding board.

Roni Wilkinson at Pen and Sword gave me the opportunity to widen my knowledge and supported the publication. Irene Moore again edited my work with care and good humour, thank you.

My apologies to anyone I have missed in individual thanks. I have attempted to verify all the facts of the story and any errors are my responsibility.

Introduction

This book is part of a series published to commemorate the First World War. It was commissioned in 2013 but might be seen as a response to a statement by Richard Denman MP who, in a speech to constituents at Carlisle Young Men's Christian Association (YMCA), said:

> *'I believe that the war has taught my constituents a good deal. It has taught Carlisle, for example, what it means to be able to work as a community. I hope that some good historian will write a little book upon Carlisle in wartime in order to keep a record of its many activities and the useful work it has done, and I think it will be found that for sanity, effectiveness, cheeriness and vigour the citizens of Carlisle have put in efforts toward this war that cannot be surpassed in any quarter of the kingdom.'*

Others will judge the quality of the historian but I hope this book records and respects the sanity, effectiveness, cheeriness and vigour of the citizens of Carlisle. The events of each year are recorded in the sequence in which they occurred. This may appear sometimes to result in a disjointed story but it reflects how things evolved at the time.

The weights and currency used in this book are those of the period. One pound (1lb) weight is equivalent to about 500g; a stone (14lbs) equates to about 6.35kg. Monetary amounts are in pounds, shillings and pence. There were 12 pence in one shilling and 20 shillings to one pound; amounts were written as £1 1s 1d; there were also halfpence (½d) and farthings (¼d). Methods of calculating relative values vary but with the system I have used an item that cost £1 in 1914 would be costing about £82 today. Something worth a shilling costs about £4 today and a penny equates to about 40p; the decimal equivalent to 10s is 50p, 1s is about 5p, and 6d is 2.5p.

Some views and comments of the time, particularly with regard to the place of Britain in relation to the Empire and the place of women in society, although both changed during the four years, may seem strange today. It is the role of the historian to recount events and attitudes as they were at the time and it is the task of the reader to accept statements within their context, reflecting on how society might have changed. Hartley's comment that 'the past is a different country, they do things differently there' frequently rings true. In many instances however, it is interesting how many of the concerns and aspirations at the beginning of the twentieth century are still unresolved and still to be achieved and the statement 'history repeats itself' may be more apposite.

CHAPTER 1

Carlisle before August 1914

Geography and short history – Population – Diocese – Local business – City women – Lord Lonsdale – Relations with Cumberland – Public health – Importance of voluntary organisations – Council responsibilities – Local press.

Carlisle, England's northern city has traditionally looked both north and south. As an English city it suffered from difficult communication with the capital, road access made difficult by the fells at Shap and the Pennines at Stainmore. Geography favoured contact with Scotland, but politics and defence determined it remained an English border stronghold.

Its geographical isolation from London and its position on the last crossing of the River Eden before encountering the wide and dangerous Solway estuary, resulted in Carlisle developing as the civic centre for the county of Cumberland controlling the crossing. The districts surrounding the city, such as Wetheral, Wigton and Stanwix, were gradually brought into its sphere of influence and became more closely aligned.

The history of conflict between England and Scotland resulted in the Border area becoming, for many centuries, a disputed territory where settlement was difficult and hazardous. Carlisle had the River Eden to act as a barrier to those attacking from the north and the Castle and Citadel rose alongside businesses to cater for the economic needs of the local populations, both English and Scots. The local economy was based on trade between the countries, particularly the passage of cattle from the Highlands to the markets in the north of England. Behind the city walls manufacturing and markets grew and banking and legal services emerged to cater for the different systems of the two countries.

It was the development of the railways during the nineteenth century that gave Carlisle a central position within a transport system which linked it more closely to the surrounding areas and other parts of both England and Scotland. The first line, opened by the Newcastle and Carlisle Company in 1836, mainly carried freight between Carlisle and the Carlisle Canal, and by 1838 across the Tyne Gap to Blaydon near Newcastle. A station for the less important passenger traffic opened in 1838 in London Road, an inconvenient distance from the city centre. Other lines opened in the following years: to Maryport in 1843, Lancaster in 1846, to Glasgow and Edinburgh on the Caledonian line in 1848 and the more important Waverley line to Edinburgh via Hawick which opened in 1862. The Citadel Station, which formed a major focus in the traffic of trains during the First World War, was built in 1847 and by 1876 all seven lines which served the city passed into the imposing station in the centre of Carlisle.

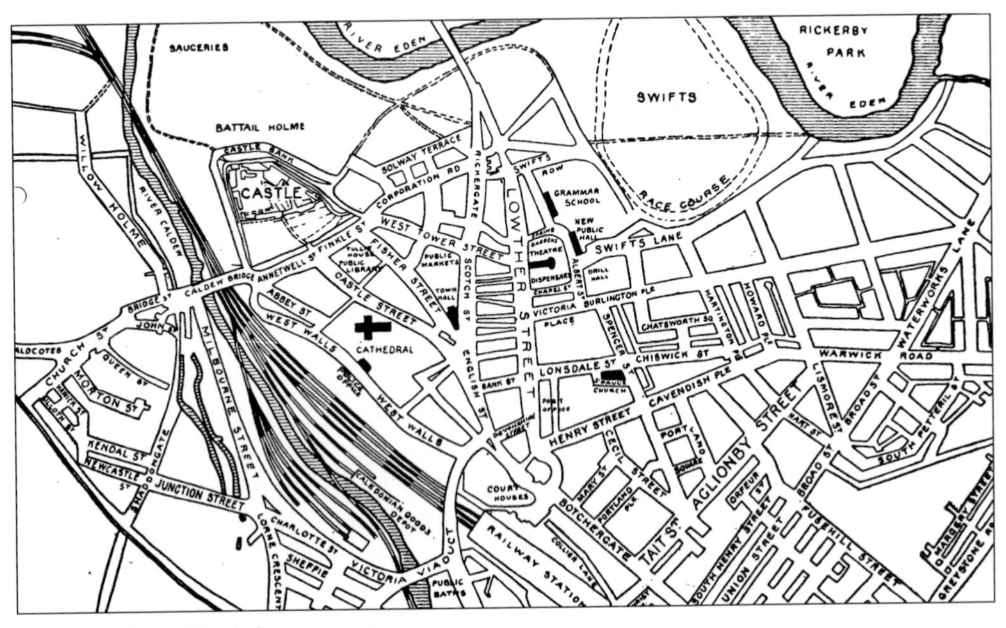

Map of Carlisle. Carlisle Library

During the nineteenth century industries developed and focused on engineering, textiles, chemicals and food processing. Kelly's Directory of 1911 described Carlisle as a city where:

> *'The trade is that of an agricultural district but it has been materially enlarged by the numerous extensive works in the neighbourhood, including that of Hudson, Scott and Sons, printers and lithographers on tin, and Cowans Sheldon and Co Ltd, Engineers. There are also other engineering works, iron foundries, breweries, tanneries and biscuit factories. The locomotive carriage and wagon repairing and cleaning depots and creosote works of the various railway companies employ over 1,000 men.'*

The population of the city in 1911 was 46,420 and by a review in 1914 was standing at 52,000. The city and surrounding area were predominantly rural and retained many of the features of a hierarchy based on land and title. A number of retired military men who had served in the Border Regiment Headquarters at the Castle remained in the area and some took on positions of responsibility, foremost among them being Major Spencer Charles Ferguson, the Mayor. His deputy, Sir Benjamin Scott, had been mayor six times and would take over the role again when Ferguson went to war.

In addition to being the cathedral city of the 67-year-old Bishop of Carlisle, the Right Reverend William Diggle, Carlisle was also home to the Right Reverend Campbell West-Watson, the Bishop of Barrow, aged just 37. He had been appointed in 1909 at the age of 32, probably the youngest priest in modern times to achieve such a position. Another clergyman in the diocese who had a house in The Abbey was Canon Hardwicke Rawnsley, a vigorous man who, while he was serving as a vicar in Cumberland, had been instrumental in helping to found the National Trust; he was a great believer in charity and was skilled at getting people to contribute to causes. He was also a poet and regular contributor to the letters pages of the local press.

The many successful local businesses provided a potential pool of management and skilled leadership. Supported by the professionals with financial and legal knowledge, the city was well placed to manage a crisis. Joseph Buck, a manufacturer of flannels, Henry Campbell, a stock and insurance broker, Thomas Charlton, a retired architect, and the Carr family, of the biscuit and flour companies, were all to feature in the running of Carlisle and the war effort in the years to come. Others, whose positions were to thrust them into the limelight, included Nicol Campbell, the station superintendent of the Citadel Station and Dr Beard, Carlisle's Medical Officer.

There were a number of prominent women too, including Miss Mabel Bardsley, daughter of the previous bishop, Mary Chance, married to Frederick a cotton manufacturer and much involved in temperance, voluntary and charity work. Miss Rosalind Henderson, a sprightly 65-year-old who was treasurer of the Charity Society. Lady Carlisle, who lived for much of the year at Brampton and was a noted member of the temperance movement and a supporter of women's rights, Beatrice Morton, wife of James, was much involved in a number of projects during the war. These women emerged as key figures.

Local churches of all denominations and many clubs and societies played their part in helping those affected by the war. Not all was positive. The Chief Constable of Carlisle, Eric Herbert de Schmid and the headmaster of Carlisle Boys' Grammar School, Charles Padel, both influential figures, were among those who were to face personal challenges brought about by hatred of those believed to have German connections.

Further away, Lord Lonsdale of Lowther, near Penrith, was a notable member of the nobility with strong links to government. He was a great sportsman, supporter of hunting, both of foxes and otters, and donated the Lonsdale Belt for boxing. He was the first president of the Automobile Association which created its livery based on Lonsdale's favourite colour, yellow. He established the Lonsdale Battalion of the Border Regiment which included many men from the city in its ranks and was an official on the Control Board which took over the breweries, pubs and off licenses in the city and surrounding area.

Carlisle became a county borough on 1 April 1914 which brought with it a greater set of responsibilities notably for education and more of the public services. This development was a source of pride, but also had teething problems, mainly to do with funding, which had to be disentangled from the accounts of the county, and was never fully resolved during the four years of conflict.

Tuberculosis was a killer and a TB dispensary opened in George Street in October 1914. Surgeries were held twice weekly in the afternoon. Dr Beard, the medical officer of health, quickly realised that those who had the disease and were still working could not get time off work to attend, so an evening clinic was provided. One hundred and twenty-four cases were notified between September and December 1914. The council agreed to pay for fifteen beds at the Blencathra Sanatorium to allow sufferers an opportunity to recuperate in fresh air. Building work to extend the sanatorium was delayed and the city had to take spaces at Meathop, near Grange-over-Sands. The treatments locally and at the sanatorium dealt only with those with symptoms of the disease. What the medical authorities were unable to do with the resources at their disposal was to advise family members and other contacts how to avoid catching the illness.

Voluntary organisations took on many tasks which are now the responsibility of local authorities or the health services. The City Dispensary was the oldest and provided an essential service to poorer families unable to afford the fees charged by doctors and who had not joined the new insurance services. In 1914 it dealt with 3,500 cases but the donations fell short of the expenditure and the dispensary accounts were in the red. One of the newest charities was The Council for Rescue and Prevention Work, set up in Carlisle in 1914 to 'rescue' women and girls who were in danger of immorality.

The Cumberland Infirmary was run by trustees and paid for by insurance or donations. The hospital had 134 beds, treating about 1,300 patients a year, plus about 4,000 out patients. The War Office requested thirty beds ready to allocate to wounded soldiers. This, the management committee concluded, would put great pressure on the facilities but they would endeavour to make provision. As the war started the number of charities increased and the population was constantly exhorted to donate money, gifts or make things to give to soldiers at home and abroad, or those just passing through the station, as well as to military families and refugees. Others contributed by joining committees to organise facilities or events, to undertake more long-term tasks, or to perform at concerts. It is to the credit of the citizens that many of them did contribute and the papers were conscientious in publishing long lists of the names of donors; many names featured frequently.

The council was also responsible for the provision of gas, electricity and water and many committee meetings were taken up with discussion of how best to improve the water supply, progress on the extension of the electricity works and the price of gas. Electricity had been installed as far as Scotby and the gas main reached as far as Great Corby. The poor quality of many of the roads had been a cause of complaint for some years and it was decided to replace the ageing granite setts on which metal cart wheels were noisy with a new material, tarmacadam. The police came under the control of the council and the Chief Constable was also the Chief Fire Officer. Equipment was primitive and the council purchased a new fire engine at the cost of £1,025, about £80,000 in 2013 values.

In the days before wireless and television, internet and email, the local papers were the main source of information. Carlisle had two newspapers, the *Cumberland News* and the *Carlisle Journal*. The *News* was a supporter of the Conservative Party; the *Journal*, the main source for this book, supported the Liberal viewpoint.

The local papers between 1914 and 1918 carried summaries of the progress of the war, lists of the volunteers signing up for duty and, later, the lists of those killed and wounded. They carried news of local battalions and were not afraid of publishing the gory details of conflicts and the effects of shells and bullets on individuals, though later censorship changed some of the styles. News of local matters, the happenings around schools, the work of the local councils, the response of businesses and individuals to the war were all carried. Church news, local hunting, fishing and farming matters, social notices and events remained to provide the ongoing rhythm of life beneath the dramas of the war and its impact.

CHAPTER 2

1914 July: Last days of normality

The Castle – Whitsun Hiring – Voluntary Aid Detachment – Red Cross – Government in London – The Irish Question – Territorial Association – Carlisle and Women's Suffrage

Life in Carlisle in July 1914 was following its usual peacetime pattern. The presence of the depot of the Border Regiment in the Castle meant that the citizens were used to the presence of the army.

The Hirings, which happened twice a year at Whitsun and again in November, was the event where farmers and farm workers met to negotiate contracts for the next six months. It usually brought thousands of men and women into the city but there was concern in 1914 that there were few men looking for farm work. Other matters covered in the papers related to cuts in council budgets for the support of the poor and the consequent possibility of local unrest. There were inspections of the local Voluntary Aid Detachments (VAD) and the War Office announced an enquiry into the working and organisation of the VAD, especially into the difficulties of co-ordinating the local branches with regard to training and how they might work together if called into action. The VAD were to be important in providing support to the authorities particularly with the provision of refreshments for troops passing through Carlisle and in local hospitals.

In parallel with the VAD, the local Red Cross Associations, both men and women's sections, were inspected and ways sought to make their potential contribution as effective as possible. They were to be mainly concerned with the establishment and running of local hospitals, should these be required.

On 14 July the *Carlisle Journal* reported a speech by Mr Asquith, the Prime Minister, in which he summarised the remaining government business:

> *'The Government decided to wind up its session as early as possible in August and to start the new session in the early winter so that the Revenue Bill might be passed to allow the grants to local authorities to be made next year. The length of the session will depend on the negotiations regarding Home Rule.'*

Irish Home Rule, to the exclusion of European tensions and events in Servia, as Serbia was then known, dominated the national news reports in both the *Carlisle Journal* and *Cumberland News* during July. The capture of 3,000 rifles smuggled into Dublin and the subsequent battle between the National Volunteers and the army was the lead item in the *Journal* on 28 July. King George V called a conference at Buckingham Palace in an attempt to resolve the matter but it ended in failure. Under a headline 'WAR CLOUDS IN THE BALKANS' the *Journal* reported:

> *'The Balkans have taken the place of the Low Countries as the cockpit of Europe. The echoes of strife between the Balkan Allies and Turkey have hardly died away and Servia, which at the end of that war found itself at conflict with its ally Bulgaria, is now confronted with the prospect of war with Austria. The new complication arises from the assassination of the Archduke Ferdinand and his consort.'*

The quarterly meeting of the Territorial Association held on Saturday, 25 July was exercised by the problem of men displaying proficiency badges to which they had no right; the state of the drill halls in a number of towns, including Carlisle; the political difficulty of allowing a drill hall to be used for an anti-tariff meeting; organising a challenge trophy for reservists; and reporting the total strength of the Territorial units in Cumberland and Westmorland as being 2,427, below the possible strength of 2,863.

The *Journal* headlines on 31 July announced 'WAR DECLARED, INVASION OF SERVIA'; 'RUSSIAN PREPARATION FOR WAR'; 'WIDE FINANCIAL PANIC, EXTRAORDINARY SLUMP IN PRICES; 'AN ANXIOUS OUTLOOK'. On 1 August the *Cumberland News* described the bombardment of Belgrade as an Austrian attempt to destroy the Servian capital. On the same day, the paper told its readers that the Irish Crisis was now overshadowed by the developments in Europe.

Domestic political matters were the subject of a meeting at Carlisle Cross on Friday, 31 July called by the Carlisle Women's Suffrage Union chaired by Miss Mabel Bardsley, daughter of the late Bishop of Carlisle. The union had come into existence in 1909 and was careful to describe itself as non-violent to differentiate itself from the more aggressive activities of others in the movement. The speaker, an Australian, received many cheers during her speech in which she pointed out the inequality and unfairness in the treatment of women. In her view the only reason they were denied the vote, and put into the same category as children, criminals, lunatics and idiots, was that they happened to come into the world not as men but as women. She contended that the war in Europe was brought about by financiers and fought by soldiers and sailors who were also denied the vote. The meeting passed a resolution demanding a government measure for the enfranchisement of women on the same basis as men.

CHAPTER 3

1914 August to December: Over by Christmas?

Calls for neutrality – Industrial peace – Border Battalions – Local volunteers – Industry and the outbreak of war – Panic buying – Citizens' League – Cumbrians in Europe – Employers offer to support recruits' families – Answering the call to arms – The Lonsdale Battalion – The problem of alcohol – Troop trains through the station – The first casualties – Martinmas Hirings – Belgian Refugees – Christmas

On Sunday, 2 August there was another well attended meeting at the Cross in Carlisle at which another resolution was passed, this time calling for neutrality in the event of the conflict in eastern Europe spreading westward. Local women, including Miss Bardsley put forward the position from the women's perspective:

> *'It was a woman's question as well as a man's question. The women with the men, they were bound together. So far as she could make out this war was brought about because one small country chose to make itself disagreeable.'*

The *Carlisle Journal* of 4 August carried an article describing the development of organisations determined to keep Britain out of a European war. The Methodist, Presbyterian, Baptist and Congregational Churches of Carlisle had signed a petition:

> *'That while this congregation remains expressing its confidence in the Government and urging a continuance of its good offices in the furtherance of peace, is of the opinion that in view of the present unfortunate European situation Great Britain should declare her absolute neutrality.'*

The Hon Richard Denman, who had been Liberal MP for Carlisle since 1910, wrote a letter dated 2 August which was published in the *Journal* of 4 August:

> *'The essential feature of this war is that the Slav races and their allies are ranged against the Teutonic races and theirs. We have no interest in the quarrel between Austria and Servia nor does Austria seem to have the worser* (sic) *cause. The question before us simply is this: "Are we gratuitously to intervene to take the part of the Slavonic civilisation against that of Germany?" To that question, whether looked at from the point of view of the Empire, of the United Kingdom or the world at large I can only answer an emphatic "No".*
>
> *If Germany then forces us into the conflict, so be it. We should then intervene and I hope decisively.'*

To the shock and surprise of many, not only in Carlisle, Britain declared war on 4 August. The *Cumberland News*, a weekly, appeared on 8 August with a page headed 'WAR NEWS'. This included reports on 'SEVEN NATIONS AT WAR'; 'THE CALL TO TERRITORIALS'; 'RAILWAYS TAKEN OVER'; 'THE RIVALS' STRENGTHS BY LAND, SEA AND AIR'; 'FOOD IN PLENTY, AN UNNECESSARY RUSH FOR STORES'; 'NO JUSTIFICATION FOR ANY RISE IN PRICES OF BREAD OR MEAT'.

For some years the Carlisle newspapers had been reporting incidents of local and national industrial unrest. Many factories including some in Carlisle had imposed restricted hours of working. Once war was declared the Trades Union Council, the General Federation of Trades Unions and the National Executive of the Labour Party issued a joint resolution intended to end all existing trade disputes and, if new difficulties arose during the war, to encourage the protagonists to make a serious attempt to reach an amicable solution before resorting to a strike or lockout. A call by the Carlisle branch of the British Socialist Party for Britain to remain neutral was reported on 8 August but on the same page was the announcement that the British Neutrality Committee in London had been disbanded.

On 4 August the paper carried an appeal from the Royal Automobile Club for motorists willing to offer the use of their vehicles for home or foreign service to give details of make and horsepower.

Many more trains than usual passed through Carlisle and local cheap excursion tickets were suspended, a hardship at the start of the holiday period for many who used the train to get to the coast at Maryport and Silloth. A group of German waiters, who had been working at the Peebles Hydro Hotel and were trying to get home to Germany were booed as the train in which they were travelling stopped in Citadel Station.

There were two local Regular Army regiments, the Border Regiment, based in Carlisle with two Regular and one Reserve Battalions and also two Territorial Army (TA) Battalions and The King's Own (Royal Lancaster) Regiment which recruited from Westmorland and had some men from Carlisle in its ranks. The Westmorland and Cumberland Yeomanry was a mounted territorial regiment under the command of the Welsh Border Mounted Brigade. The headquarters were in Penrith but D Squadron was based in Carlisle with men from the city, and also some from Wigton and Alston.

The peacetime deployment of British regiments was to have one Regular battalion overseas and the other at home. The Border Regiment 1st Battalion (1 Border) was in Maymyo, Burma, the 2nd Battalion (2 Border) was at Pembroke Dock. The King's Own (Royal Lancaster), Regiment 1st Battalion (1 King's Lancaster) was in Dover and landed in France on 23 August. For the Expeditionary Force to have any hope of success it was these Regular troops that were needed in Belgium and France, not the enthusiastic but inexperienced men lining up hopefully at Carlisle Castle.

Some old and semi-experienced soldiers were available. The National Reservists had completed seven years full-time service with the colours and then a further five in the Reserve. Others had signed up for six years in the Special Reserve, which began with six months full-time training and three to four weeks annual training. Many regiments had Territorial battalions where the men attended weekly training and an annual summer camp. A key difference between the Reserves and Territorial men was that the former could be sent to serve abroad, usually as drafts to replace men wounded or taken ill; the latter could be called upon for full-time service but were not obliged to serve overseas unless they specifically volunteered.

The challenge facing the War Office with the sudden declaration of war was to get the Regular troops to France and ensure that there were replacements, particularly for those serving in India and other parts of the Empire. Carlisle's place in the rail network meant that the city's Citadel Station witnessed the passage of trains bringing Scottish Regiments south.

August was the month in which Reserve and Territorial battalions carried out their annual training camps. Border TA units caught trains at the Citadel Station on Saturday, 1 August to attend their annual camp at Caernarfon in North Wales, but no sooner had they arrived at their destination than they were put back on the train to Carlisle.

Local groups offered assistance; Boy Scouts were organised to carry out support duties such as acting as messengers, meeting trains to give refreshments to the troops, and acting as guides to soldiers in the city. Members of the Cumberland Motor Cycle Club volunteered to act as dispatch riders when messages had to be carried further than a boy scout could manage. Local citizens, including the Mayor and one of the local members of parliament volunteered to rejoin their regiments. The day after war was declared excited crowds thronged the streets to see the men of 4 Border Territorials arrive. The Carlisle Company paused in their departure to join in the laying up of the colours in the Cathedral. This old tradition of lodging the prized flags in the safe keeping of the church saw the Dean of Carlisle accompanied by other church dignitaries, receive the colours of the 2, 3 and 4 Border Battalions, those of 2 Battalion having been sent from Pembroke Dock. The colour parties and church dignitaries progressed through the Cathedral and the battalions returned to the Castle and Drill Hall to continue their preparations.

There was much uncertainty about the effect of the war on local industry and in the second week the papers carried calming reports about the intentions of most of the larger companies. Hudson Scott, the metal box printers, were continuing to work as normal, but were worried that supplies of raw materials would be reduced. Alexander Morton, textile manufacturers, produced coloured material but most of

2 Border Colours at laying up ceremony in Carlisle Cathedral 5 August 1914.
Ashley Kendall

Colour Party Carlisle Cathedral 5 August 1914. Ashley Kendall

their dyes came from Germany so they too were concerned about future sources of supply. Another textile company, R.R. Buck, was also affected, this time by the cutting off of supplies of yarn from the continent. Trade in the other direction was damaged for hat makers Carrick and Sons who had to cancel deliveries to Germany and Belgium. Todd and Sons manufactured cloth and although they had lost their domestic trade, were producing khaki for the army and 'anticipated that this would keep the works going for some time as orders are required urgently'. Cowans, Sheldon and Company, manufacturers of heavy cranes and railway equipment, were fairly confident that they could continue to work full time, but about forty of their men had gone off with the Territorials. Carr's had good stocks of flour and anticipated maintaining supplies of their biscuits. Coal had been in short supply because many of the rail lines were congested with trains carrying troops around the country.

There was some panic buying in the shops, particularly of flour, sugar and foodstuffs. Concern that imports would be reduced or cut off entirely led people to try to store up essential items. As a result some tradesmen closed their shops and wholesalers either announced that they had no further stocks, or put their prices up; a stone (6.5kg) of flour rose from about 1s 9d (9p) to 2s 6d (12.5p) during the week. Supplies of Danish butter, the main source, was ended, resulting in further price rises of remaining supplies and the price of Irish bacon went up by thirty-three per cent. Articles in the press attempted to encourage people to stop panic buying but it took a few weeks before prices stabilised.

On Tuesday, 11 August the Deputy Mayor, Sir Benjamin Scott, presided at a meeting attended by most of the notable people of the city. It had been called following a deputation to him the previous Friday where a number of people expressed willingness to help with the war effort locally, but didn't know what they could do. The difficulty of managing volunteers was discussed and a resolution was proposed, seconded and agreed which said:

> *'That this meeting is of the opinion that a League of Carlisle Citizens be formed to utilise the services of such citizens of the city as are desirous of assisting the authorities in any capacity in which their services are required.'*

Sir Benjamin, having been elected as chairman of the League, was careful to point out that its work should not clash with that of the military authorities. He urged everyone present to encourage their friends of military age, especially those who were unmarried, to enlist. Two secretaries were appointed and offices established at 7 The Crescent, near the Court House and station. A notice was to be placed in newspapers describing the League and what it would be doing and asking for people wishing to help to sign the register.

Another organisation that would play a large part in the war was quickly into action. The Red Cross was charged with identifying possible buildings to be turned into hospitals and convalescent homes. The first two were established at the County Girls' High School where part of the building was adapted, and at the Chadwick Memorial School, which had been an Industrial School for 200 Catholic boys. In both places ladies of the district rallied round to clean and prepare the rooms. Many of those who volunteered came from homes where servants usually carried out the menial duties, but the women were to prove capable of doing it themselves. Among the volunteers at the Chadwick Memorial were a widow and daughter of the Carr biscuit family. Maud Carr, widow of James, had been a volunteer at the Cumberland Infirmary and knew how hospitals worked. She and her niece Dorothy, daughter of Theodore Carr, worked at the Chadwick, at first scrubbing and cleaning but later as assistants nursing the men.

During the third week of August members of local army units received instructions to muster but the War Office and regimental orders had not arrived to move them on. Members of the National and Special Reserves left for Pembroke Dock to join 2 Border there. Although men were presenting themselves at the Castle to volunteer, the Border Regiment was not accepting new recruits so they were being passed to other regiments and sent to Aldershot.

Lord Lonsdale had spent the summer on the Continent at Deauville. He and his family were back home at Lowther Castle, near Penrith but his yellow Rolls Royce was among 183 cars commandeered on the dockside at Le Havre for war work in France. He was in contact with the War Office trying to get permission to raise a battalion.

Local papers carried reports of Cumbrians attempting to return from holidays or business on the Continent. The *Cumberland News* on 5 September said that the sister of Mr Robson, a confectioner in

Rickergate, had returned to Carlisle from Tournai, where she had been living for twelve years. An artist at the Hudson Scott Works, Mr Molyneux, was a confirmed prisoner of the Germans. James Long, the writer of a weekly column in the *Carlisle Journal* on farming, was detained with a large number of British, Australian and Canadians as they were trying to cross the border from Switzerland to look at farming practice in Switzerland, Alsace and Luxembourg.

A more dramatic and frightening experience was that of Mrs Whitely and her children whose home was in Mayson Street, Currock. She was in Hamburg visiting her brother and had delayed her departure from 28 July. She got on board a ship bound for Newcastle three days later but the crew was suddenly ordered to unload its cargo of sugar so she returned to her brother's house to wait. She discovered that his employer and his parents had all committed suicide as they feared that their business would be ruined if war broke out. When war with Britain was declared on 4 August the situation in Hamburg became worse. All signs and anything associated with Britain was destroyed, the Captain of the *Juno*, the ship she was supposed to travel on, told her that they could not leave until German mobilisation was complete.

The American Consul advised all Britons to leave the city and make their way to Denmark. They managed to get to Altona just outside Hamburg on the Prussian border but here they were taken prisoner and placed in a small cell. The following morning the guards asked if Mrs Whitely was able to pay for food, and when she said she couldn't she and the children were given some rough black bread and coffee. Rescue came in the shape of the local Commissioner of Police who said that they should be released immediately, given something better to eat and sent on their way. Arriving at Esjberg, they were delighted to find a ship bound for England and travelled on it to Harwich, from where they managed to get back to Carlisle.

News about Mr Molyneux, the artist employed by Hudson Scott, was received by his mother from the wife of a fellow prisoner. About eight men were being held in a beer garden in Bentheim, Lower Saxony to the north of Essen, and charged three shillings a day, but not everyone had money so they pooled what they had. The Foreign Office in London had been asked to send money to the men. William Bulman wrote to his wife to reassure her that he was well and that it was very quiet in Vienna.

Firms in and around the city offered to keep places open and in some cases to make up salaries for those joining up by adding to Army pay, particularly to those married men who had gone to serve with the Territorials. In the same notice they announced that if because of economic and business reasons it became necessary to reduce the numbers employed then young unmarried men of military age would be unlikely to be retained. Buck and Sons announced to their workers that it was probable that there would have to be a reduction in the number employed and encouraged single young men to apply to join the army; those who did would be paid an allowance to maintain their salary. Another of the engineering works undertook to pay the rents of families left behind thus allowing the whole of the Army allowance to be spent on food and clothing. The North Eastern Railway Company made similar provision for its employees by undertaking to allow families to continue to occupy company houses.

German sailors taken off ships in the Tyne arrived in Citadel Station on their way to Lancaster. A large crowd gathered but during the hour the men were in the station waiting for their connecting train the platform was barricaded.

The individual members of the Territorial Battalions in Barrow, 4 and 5 Border, were asked to volunteer for service abroad. They could opt to remain Home Service only but about ninety per cent of both battalions, with virtually every officer, offered to serve overseas if required. As a first move, both battalions were ordered to join the Home Counties Division at Sittingbourne, Kent.

After a slower start than some other places Carlisle men flocked to volunteer at the Castle during the week of 10 September. The report in the *Journal* was the first which praised the response of the young men of the district:

> *'There may not have been the clash of arms or the anxiety and excitement of siege or battle but the Castle has witnessed scenes of a kind which are unparalleled in its long history and the citizens have been stirred by the sight of hundreds of young men ready at the call of their country to give the greatest service that men can be called upon to perform. At the outbreak of the war recruiting proceeded at a moderate pace but the men of the North, having realised the seriousness of the danger which threatens the country*

began to flock into the city and as group after group reached the Castle their arrival aroused increasing interest.

'The stream of recruits is flowing steadily and the charge that the men of the North are apathetic can no longer be brought against them... Every night this week batches of about a hundred men have arrived at the station and marched to the Castle.

'Information as to the number of recruits is withheld at the recruiting office and reticence on this subject can be understood. As to the number of men who are drafted to distant regiments and other stations, it is impossible to form an estimate but this number is considerable...The 6th Battalion (Service) of the Border Regiment is complete and another is rapidly being built up to swell Lord Kitchener's Army for service abroad.

'A splendid class of young men is now trooping to the colours. The majority of them are men of fine physique strong limbed, active and what is more of cheerful disposition and full of determination to do their part in the country's struggle. That is where the volunteer is superior to the conscript as a fighting man. Here women look on with thoughts of their own husbands and sons.'

Tents were erected on the Swifts and all round Carlisle squads were learning drill and waiting to be sent off to a training camp. At this stage many of the Carlisle volunteers were sent to fill spaces in regiments up and down the country; twenty-two men went to join a Hussar Regiment.

About 100 men from Carr's Biscuit factory answered their country's call. Thirty men from Hudson Scott were drilling in the company's yard having decided to join up together. Twenty men from Cowans, Sheldon and Co marched to the Artillery recruiting office to enlist in the 4th (East Lancashire) Brigade of the Royal Field Artillery, leaving behind a further thirty-five who were going to enlist in other regiments. Thirty men signed on from Mortons and another thirty left Holme Head Works. Ten men enlisted from Tyers, bringing the total from the company to about twenty-two. Carricks put up a notice offering to pay 10s to the wives or dependent mothers of men signing up; as a direct result twelve men volunteered during the week.

It wasn't only local businesses that provided opportunities for men

Border Regiment recruits physical training with an audience in Bitts Park.
Ashley Kendall

to decide that they wanted to serve together. Nineteen players from the Carlisle Rugby Club joined 4 Border at Barrow and volunteered for service overseas. A number of Cumberland Motor Cycle Club members joined the colours and at its meeting on 5 August the club suggested its members join up as despatch riders and cancelled all meetings planned for the year.

The rush of recruits put a huge strain on the recruiting and training system. Instead of leaving home in the morning and not being seen by their families until they appeared in a training squad around the city, men were given a nominal day of service when they signed up, and were then sent home to await being called back to join a squad. A number of the men had been sent home having expressed a desire to join a local 'Pals' Battalion. These 'locally raised' battalions were intended to encourage men from a locality or from similar backgrounds to volunteer and serve together to make up the 100,000 men required for 'Kitchener's Army' . The first of these, the 10th Battalion, Royal Fusiliers and the 17th Battalion, King's Liverpool, had been established in late August.

A large contingent of men arrived from Tyneside and was sent back, but between 150 and 200 arrived on 7 September from Tyneside and Darlington. The better management of the flow of recruits allowed those in charge at the Castle to organise accommodation and training more effectively, with a steady population of men in the Castle around 500, and a further 700 under canvas at the Swifts and more billeted in drill halls and public houses. The War Office's sudden change in height and chest requirement, raising the standard for height by 3ins to 5ft 6ins and the chest measurement by 1.5ins to 35.5ins meant that a number of otherwise quite fit men were suddenly unable to enlist.

The Citizens' League had taken the details of nearly 500 men volunteering for the proposed Lonsdale Battalion and also helped the Army in dealing with the flood of recruits. Although there had been a good number of recruits from the city there was concern that the number from the surrounding area was only a small proportion of those who might be expected to volunteer, and so a sub-committee was set up to organise recruitment in the districts around Carlisle.

Army stocks were slow in arriving and the men had to make do with their civilian clothes, which were not surviving the hard wear to which they were subjected in training. One committee member, Mr T.W. Carr, offered his premises in Devonshire Street as a depot for the collection of clothes and magazines for distribution to the soldiers.

The increased number of soldiers in the city was putting pressure on places of relaxation. Twenty-seven year old Robert Chance, who with his father ran the family cotton factory, wrote in the *Journal* to ask for help in giving more entertainment opportunities for the soldiers. The Boys Brigade Institute on Abbey Street and the Wesley Hall in Fisher Street were taken over but needed furniture and easy chairs which, it was hoped, the readers of the paper could spare. The British Women's Temperance Association collected magazines and paper for writing letters and the staff of the Boys' Brigade and Wesley Hall opened the centres each evening and on Sunday afternoons. Training was carried out in Bitts Park and the men had lemonade provided for them by Mrs Bardsley, widow of the late bishop, and her daughter.

Not all attempts at entertaining troops were viewed as being positive. Edwin Blackwell, a member of the Temperance Society wrote a long letter complaining about the practice of 'treating' soldiers to drinks. Quoting from a report by the London Commissioner of Police that 'scarcely a train left the city with any sober men on board' he appealed to the people of Carlisle:

> *'When will Englishmen learn wisdom in such matters and recognise that no greater disservice can be done to our soldiers and recruits than to weaken at such times both their moral and physical fibre by alcoholic indulgence when every fraction of self control and self respect counts in the creation of the morale and condition of the men entering upon the tremendous ordeal which now confronts them?'*

Sunday, 13 September saw the departure of 8 Border to a camp at Lewes in Sussex. The military nature of the event was slightly marred as the men were marching in their civilian clothes. Huge crowds gathered to cheer the battalion as they left the Castle in the evening, headed by local bands, and marched down Castle Street, English Street and Court Square en route to the station. The crowds in Court Square cheered loudly as the men passed through the throng to the strains of *Rule Britannia*.

On the following morning men of 7 Border marched to the Castle and, after being issued with boots, returned to their camp to prepare to depart for Devonshire. Over 1,100 men set off later from the camp on the Swifts to march, again in civilian clothes, to the station, accompanied by a great cheering crowd. Those who waited to see more action were rewarded by the first sight of men with uniforms and rifles leaving the Castle when 204 men marched to the station to join 6 Border at Grantham. In total over two days more than 2,000 men left the city and their departure left accommodation free in the Castle for recruits who had been awaiting the call to present themselves.

The next group to muster at the Castle were the men who were to comprise 9 Border. They received the telegrams on Sunday, 13 September, as the men of 8 Border were marching to the station. The confusion at the start of the war came to the surface with these men as many of them thought they had signed up to join a local Pals Battalion. It was known throughout the city that Lord Lonsdale was still attempting to get permission to recruit a local battalion and although, as the papers reported, the men had signed and attested their willingness to serve in the Border Regiment, there was some ill-feeling that they had been 'collared' to serve in other than the yet to be recruited Lonsdale Battalion. The Army authorities explained that the concept of a Pals battalion would be honoured in the 9 Border with friends serving together.

Men arrived from all parts of the counties of Cumberland and Westmorland and within four days 1,300 were assembled described as being:

> *'men of athletic build, drawn from business and commercial establishments and offices. Without exception they are men of better education and circumstances than the majority of men who have hitherto been seen in the ranks.'*

They had been drilling in their home towns in preparation for being called into service and the process of forming platoons and companies continued. On Thursday, 17 September, the recruits were marched in driving rain along the Warwick Road, most of them wearing only their civilian suits without overcoats, and so returned to camp soaked through. Their clothes dried as the men wore them to be drilled in better weather during the afternoon and after a parade in the evening over 1,000 were marched to the station and put on trains to take them to the training grounds at Salisbury. No band was available to lead them but the men sang all the way along Lowther Street and through Court Square to the trains.

The lack of space in the Castle and the increasing need to accommodate recruits led the army authorities to order the families of regular soldiers living in the married quarters to move out so that the accommodation could be turned into dormitories. This was happening at many depots and barracks across the country but the army gave no extra support to the women whose husbands were serving in the regular battalions. The sudden eviction obviously placed many in a dilemma as housing was already in short supply in Carlisle and an appeal was put out for people willing to provide space for the women and children.

The departure of the three battalions and other recruits rather dampened the 17 September opening ceremony of the Skating Rink Soldiers' Club, described as a 'fairy palace'. Although many of the men whom it was intended to serve were assembling to march to the station, a few managed to avail themselves of the facilities and those present at the opening hoped that as new recruits arrived they would find it useful.

Recruitment for the Pals, or Locally Raised Battalions to give them their official title, had begun towards the end of August with the first being fully manned and entering camp in the first days of September. These battalions were not funded by the War Office but were the responsibility of those who raised them who had to provide accommodation, clothing and equipment until the battalion was judged efficient and taken onto the army strength.

Lord Lonsdale had contacted the War Office in mid-August before the locally raised experiment began, but was told he could not raise his own battalion, he had 'to allow the army to carry out recruiting in the normal way'. Not being one to give up, he persisted and by 15 September the local Territorial Association were reported in the *Journal* as meeting to discuss arrangements for recruiting and equipping 'The Lonsdale Battalion of The Border Regiment':

> *'Lord Kitchener had now put it to the Associations to raise, feed, clothe, house and pay a New Army and had laid down certain*

lines upon which to work. Anyone who knew Lord Kitchener knew he was a man who liked people to act and act without going into minor little questions.'

The provision of uniforms was a problem because of the lack of khaki cloth. Colonel Main was unable to find anyone able to supply blue, the locally preferred colour, in less than four weeks. He did find a source of grey serge from a mill in Kendal for the price allowed by the War Office. There was concern that one town would monopolise the supply, and therefore the benefit, so an invitation was opened to all manufacturers to supply material, which could be made up by local tailors, including those working independently in the villages. It was decided to centre the battalion in one place, with most of the men being away from their homes, but there would be three recruiting centres with 500 men being the target for Carlisle, 200 from Workington and 300 from Kendal. Mr Frederick Chance, a cotton manufacturer from Carlisle who was on the committee warned that, while he was sure manufacturers would support recruitment, some had already lost men to the army and the needs of local industry had to be borne in mind. Lord Lonsdale communicated the plans to London.

Recruitment was organised by the Citizens' League from their new office in English Street. The *Journal* of 25 September said that although the names of about 500 men had been taken on the Monday it was likely that not all would be viewed as being eligible as:

'The object was to confine the Battalion to men of a particular type as regards education and calling.'

Although not specific about what type of education and calling was being looked for, the paper listed thirty-eight occupations already represented including commercial travellers and insurance agents, farmers, stationer's assistant, signal maker, piano tuner, florist, dining car attendant, motor car driver, cook, waiter, hotel boots, bricklayers and plasterers.

The papers kept up a supply of news about the Border battalions after they left Carlisle. In the 22 September edition of the *Journal* there was a story about 5 Border in Barrow. Reflecting the regimental march,

D'ye ken John Peel based on a ballad about a Border huntsman, Private MacDonald was given a fox cub and trained him to follow him and to ride on the handlebars of his bicycle. 'Winkles' as the cub was called, had been taken by Private MacDonald to Barrow where he was adopted as the mascot to the battalion.

The churches played a large part in supporting troops from among their congregations and their families. One minister visited every family of his congregation to give a letter he had written to each man and present him with a bible.

Carlisle's place on the main line between London and Glasgow and a major junction meant that as hospital trains travelled from the south they stopped at the station. The first detailed reports told the readers about two trains which passed through the station on their way to Aberdeen. They were carrying 200 soldiers wounded in the fighting at Mons who had crossed to Southampton and after treatment there were put on trains to Scotland. Dr Barnes, as Medical Officer for Carlisle, had been contacted by the Medical Services Director in Southampton asking if the men could be provided with refreshments while the train was stopped in Citadel Station. About seventy members of the three Carlisle detachments of the Red Cross arrived at the station in uniform and, with the assistance of local Boy Scouts and staff from the County Hotel, served out Bovril, Oxo, tea, coffee, cocoa, sandwiches, biscuits, fruit and cigarettes. The men were also given postcards to send to families and in return they handed over souvenirs of their experiences including bullet cartridges, buttons and shell fragments. The event was something of a civic occasion as the train was met by the Mayor, the Chief Constable, the Deputy Mayor and local doctors.

With the departure of the Border battalions life in the city returned to something approaching normality and the camps on the Swifts and the Sauceries were virtually deserted. Recruits were arriving in small numbers, the recruiting of men for the Lonsdale Battalion continued at the Citizens' League office and the normal recruiting office reopened for the Border Regiment at the Castle.

The local Territorial Association decided to base the Lonsdale Battalion at Blackhall Racecourse, the Swifts site judged to be too liable to flooding to provide a semi-permanent camp. The racecourse was well drained, provided space for drilling and manoeuvres and there was some accommodation for the men to sleep as well as office space. Equipment was collected at the site and men were told individually when to report to avoid overcrowding. Once again the press gave a detailed description of the way the accommodation was to be organised and included small details, including the fact that 180 pillows had been delivered by the Citizens' League with more to follow.

All types of people in Carlisle gave money or items to support the war effort, or alleviate the distress of others. The Citizens' League, comprised mainly of business people and professional and clerical workers, served as a co-ordinating body for many of the activities, as well as contributing items from individuals and business members. Others, including churches, held local collections; the staff at Citadel Station agreed to give a regular amount from their weekly pay to the Carlisle Distress Fund; the Carlisle Pillow League met regularly at Mr Holywell's grocers shop in Lowther Street to stuff pillows for soldiers, at first with paper and then with chaff provided by local farmers. The Women's Temperance Association and the Rockcliffe Working Guild met to make clothes for soldiers and their families. Teasdale and Company, at their confectioners in South Vale, provided sugar to be boiled with fruit brought in by individuals to make jam for distribution to those in need.

Lord Lonsdale reported to the Territorial Association that finally he had an agreement to the raising of the Lonsdale Battalion but the War Office was determined that there had to be no overlap with the work being done at the Castle. He had undertaken to sign the papers on behalf of the committee agreeing to the formation of the battalion, and the War Office had telegraphed recruiting officers in Cumberland and Westmorland telling them not to interfere with the formation of the battalion; Captain Percy Machell of Crackenthorpe near Appleby, agreed to his name being put forward as commanding officer. Work to prepare Blackwell Camp went on apace with Lord Lonsdale paying to have a secure water supply and Mr Barker from the Great Central Hotel being awarded the contract for catering.

Another two hospital trains arrived late in the evening of 22 September and the wounded soldiers were again provided with refreshments. Not all the men who had once lived in Carlisle were going to return, however. The first man born in Carlisle to be killed was James

Ward, a member of 1st Battalion, King's Royal Rifle Corps (KRRC) who died on 16 September 1914; the next day William Dewars, another Carlisle man with KRRC, was killed. The third casualty was Thomas Graham serving with the 1st Battalion King's (Liverpool) Regiment who died on 20 September leaving parents living in Randall Street and a pregnant wife. The baby, named Thomasina, was born after her father was killed but she only survived for a few days.

Individuals joining the Lonsdales were named in the papers, including some with a sporting reputation such as George McCumiskey who had played for Carlisle United and Thomas Hodgkinson, a Carlisle and Cumberland county rugby player who was a manager at Hudson Scotts factory. Some of the men were old soldiers bringing experience to leaven the enthusiasm of the other volunteers. The numbers volunteering slowed during the month and there was a feeling in Carlisle that if recruiting to the battalion had begun in August it would have been full in days. Instead many of the keen volunteers who presented themselves early were put into other battalions of the Border Regiment, or sent to regiments in other parts of the country.

The effect of the war on business caused difficulty particularly to those who depended on trade with Germany. Some were unsure whether to pay all their bills but a letter read to the members of the Chamber of Commerce at their meeting on 7 October made it very clear that although some companies had German associations, if they were based in Britain then traders and manufacturers should be paying bills by the due date and were not protected from paying because of the German connection. Although the railways were under pressure to keep the trains running carrying troops to and from the south there was an appeal for experienced men, with skills as telegraphists, inspectors and engine drivers to volunteer for duty to keep the railways running in France.

During the month 4 Border Territorials were given leave prior to travelling to India and from there to Burma to relieve the Regulars of 1 Border who were to return to Britain and then go to France.

Accommodation for troops was in short supply so wooden huts were built, first outside the Castle walls with others planned for the Castle Square. There were continued and regular appeals to men in the city and surrounding areas to volunteer. Canon Hardwicke Rawnsley, a frequent correspondent to the press, wrote a long letter exhorting men to consider their position as their contracts with farmers ended at the coming Martinmas Hirings. He urged them to think about the need to serve against Germany rather than remaining in farm work. He suggested that the girls in the county should urge their men friends to enlist:

> *'Many girls at these Martinmas Hirings will be meeting the men of their heart; let them take matters into their own hands and tell the men straight out that their duty is to join the colours to fight for right and honour, to save the Empire from ruin, to rid Europe of the mailed fist forever and the world from a military domination as ruthless in spirit as it is barbarous in operation.'*

There was increased concern over the relatively slow rate of recruiting to the Lonsdale Battalion. The Citizens' League set up meetings at

Recruits of 11 Border (Lonsdale) Battalion at the racecourse 19 November 1915. Ashley Kendall

Carlisle Cross on 17 and 18 October. On the first night twenty-three men volunteered, making the total for Carlisle up to 345 of the 500 required. The new recruits were marched out of the city to the camp at the racecourse. The onlookers were impressed that the men were being drilled and led by Corporal Hodgkinson, the Carlisle rugby player who had been an early volunteer.

The men of 2 Border who had landed at Zeebrugge on 6 October were involved in heavy action near Ypres just two weeks later. The first reports reached Carlisle as wounded men passed through the station on their way to hospital in Scotland. One man told his wife of an apparent trick by some Germans who appeared with a white flag, but when men of the Borders went to take the surrender they were fired upon with many killed. One report said only 400 men were left to answer the roll call. The city and county were comparatively fortunate in that of the 124 men who died between 20 and 30 October only two originated from the city and a further nine from the counties of Cumberland and Westmorland.

Recruitment had slowed to a point that was causing some concern, more men were taken on to the strength of the Lonsdale battalion and a recruiting campaign was held in the city and across the county. Canon Rawnsley again wrote to the press:

> *'We in our quiet districts in the north have not yet realised what this war is about and how the real issue is not between France and Germany or Russia and Germany but between Great Britain and Germany. On the men of Cumberland I urge that the blood of the 600 men of the Border Regiment who with their eight officers after an eight-day battle on the left wing fell like heroes rather than leave their post, cries from the ground to bid our young Cumberland men fill their places and fight as they fought for home and Empire.'*

The appeals were not successful as only forty or fifty recruits of the 2,000 men of military age at the hirings volunteered.

Belgian troops were seen at the station when 200 of them who had been injured were given refreshments as they made their way to Aberdeen:

'A more striking set of men has seldom gone through the station. They seem to represent the stern realities, the hardships and the sufferings of a terrible campaign borne with splendid fortitude. Yet they were not the worst sufferers. Their injuries were regarded as minor and they were able to sit up and travel in ordinary cars but several heads were swathed in bandages and many arms were carried in slings. Only two days before they had been in the fighting at Ypres...

'These were not soldiers in spick and span khaki. They were in dingy navy blue uniforms and their boots and trousers were thick with mud up to their knees. ..

'If their clothes bespoke rough life, their faces were even more eloquent. Their skin was tanned almost brown and every face had upon it many days growth of hair. Some of them had short curly beards black or fair and the hirsute growth of others were in the stage which can be described as being neither bristle or orderly hair, their general appearance being of rural workers who had neglected their personal appearance for nearly a month. Yet in spite of signs of neglect their faces were bright and intelligent and many of their eyes sparkled with pleasure at the reception they had in Carlisle Station.'

The Belgian soldiers who had been seen at the station were not the first of their countrymen to arrive in Carlisle. Germany invaded Belgium on 4 August, after the king had refused to allow them free passage through his country. It was while the Belgians held up the German advance for eleven days that the British Army prepared the Expeditionary Force. On 16 August the Liège forts fell and the Germans were able to resume the Schlieffen Plan, although by now it was behind schedule and France and Britain had taken the opportunity to prepare for war.

The German army marched unopposed through Brussels on 20 August and the Belgian army retreated to the forts around Antwerp, intending to harry the German army and distract it from the advance into France. Antwerp fell on 10 October and thereafter Germany effectively held most of Belgium. The bravery of the Belgian army and the stories of atrocities committed by the Germans which were widely publicised in the British press, and retold in local papers like the *Cumbrian News* and *Carlisle Journal*, led the public to react sympathetically to the hardship of the civilian population so when the first refugees arrived in Folkestone they were immediately greeted with offers of help. The ad hoc support was quickly organised nationally by Lady Lugard's Hospitality Committee which set up a structure under which local committees, including those in Carlisle, Cumberland and Westmorland, functioned.

An early response to the crisis was a letter in the *Cumberland News* of 11 September in which readers were told that members of the Society of Friends (Quakers) were offering to take Belgian families into their homes. They hoped that others would participate to allow a group of refugees to come to Carlisle where they would be able to keep in touch with friends.

The city had already subscribed £800 to the relief fund in London when the *Journal* of 9 October included an account of the suffering of a family of Belgian refugees who had passed through Carlisle and arrived in Workington. It told of their taking shelter in Louvain, fleeing when the Germans arrived and becoming separated from the rest of their party. They were imprisoned and witnessed the shooting of two priests, and four other people disappeared. 'They wandered around for eight weeks witnessing death and destruction before they could escape to Britain'.

Three days later the *Journal* was reporting that the flood of refugees was such that the War Refugees Committee could not cope with the numbers and was hoping that local Relief Boards and Citizens' Leagues would take on the task. Although the offer of individual homes, cottages and rooms was welcome this would not meet the demand so a census of local accommodation to create a list of rooms available in each city and district around Carlisle was the only way to meet the needs of the refugees.

On the morning of Friday, 16 October passengers and workers at the station witnessed the plight first hand. Two trains carrying over 1,000 refugees passed through the station on their way to Scotland. The first train arrived at 10.15am and people on the platform bought food and fruit from the stalls to give to the travellers. The arrival of the second train at noon was greeted by the Deputy Mayor and Town Clerk who organised refreshments, again supplemented by gifts from those waiting for other trains. The next two trains of refugees which came through in the early hours of Saturday morning were given refreshments by the Silver Grill, arranged by the Deputy Mayor.

An individual act of kindness also reported in the *Carlisle Journal* was that of a taxi driver who took Mabel Graham and her father to the station to help a Belgian electrician and his family. The Belgian had a job waiting for him in Peebles but he was stuck overnight in Carlisle and Miss Graham, who could speak French, was called to assist by the station staff. The Grahams decided that the best course of action was to take the man, his wife and baby back to their house in Howard Place. The taxi driver refused to take payment for his work.

The Deputy Mayor convened a meeting of the most influential people in Carlisle four days later; eighty-one names were listed in the *Journal* as having attended. Individuals offered help, the district nurses would visit all the families, Canon Rawnsley had approached Mr Mason Scott, a director of a building company, owner of the Crown and Mitre in the city and rugby international who had just bought Rickerby House. Mr Scott had already offered the mansion to the Red Cross as a hospital but if they did not want it he was happy to have it used for refugees. Canon Rawnsley, never one to miss an opportunity, was already in London and sent a telegram to say that he had just been told that the Red Cross did not want the mansion and so it could be used for refugees. In addition he had been in touch with the chairman of the National Committee for Belgian Refugees and had obtained application forms for the Carlisle committee to complete, when it was appointed.

On 25 October members of Charlotte Street Congregational Church decided to take action on their own. The Reverend Summers received an offer from Hudson Scott, metal box manufacturers, of four cottages in James Street to house refugee families. A committee was formed, some ladies of the church were appointed to arrange supplies of food and furniture, the pastor and three men undertook to ensure that the properties were cleaned and painted. The Belgian families arrived as part of a large group on Thursday, 29 October as the minute book recorded:

> *'A never to be forgotten scene, the refugees arrived in the city just as they had been driven from their homes by German troops.'*

They arrived by train having been escorted from London by the Bishop of Barrow, Mrs Morton, wife of the textiles manufacturer, and Miss Henderson, the secretary of the Carlisle Charity Society.

At the committee meeting on 4 November the pastor reported that he had been told that no more Belgian refugees would be arriving. The *Journal* on 3 November passed on the news about changes in the type of support needed in a report headed 'OUR BELGIAN GUESTS; HOW THEY ARE HOUSED; MANY OFFERS OF HELP' the report began:

> *'The number of refugees in Carlisle under the care of the committee is thirty-six but there are others in the city who have come privately making the total about sixty. Some of the Belgians who arrived last Thursday are busy in helping prepare the mansion at Rickerby which will probably be ready this weekend for the reception of about fifty refugees, whilst number 3 Victoria Place is being prepared by the congregation of St Mary's Church to accommodate about fifteen others.'*

Bows and flowers in the colours of the Belgian flag were made by all the school children, girls clubs and societies for sale across the city. The papers recorded that nobody could be seen who was not wearing the Belgian colours. A total of £400 (over £35,000 in 2013) was raised for Belgian refugees. At least one Belgian was quick to take advantage of local opportunities. George Bulke, who arrived on a Thursday, was given a trial with Carlisle United reserves in a match with Eskdale Juniors at Brunton Park two days later.

That same afternoon the first residents were present at a house warming laid on by the Refugee Committee at Rickerby. Local people provided musical entertainment; Bertram Lewis, a local violinist and conductor played the national anthems of the Allies, Miss Kellet, one of the daughters of the superintendent at the Post Office, sang.

The secretary of the Women's Temperance Association, Isobel Boyd, wrote to the paper warning against treating the Belgian refugees to drinks as they were used to weaker beer. Social differences were noted and explained in December:

> *'It was noticed at the Citadel Station the other day on the arrival of a party of Belgian refugees that some of the women on leaving the train were carrying their hats. Onlookers had concluded that the train had stopped before they realised that they were at the end of*

> *their journey... The women showed no disposition to put on their hats. According to Mr Clive Holland who recently lectured in Carlisle, the possession of a hat by a Belgian woman – to be carried in the hand and not worn on the head – is a mark of respectability.'*

The quiet life, away from the stresses of war was helping to improve the health of the refugees. The men who were of military age had registered with the Belgian military authorities in London and were waiting to be called up. Some of the qualifications and experience of the men would be difficult to fit into the industries of the city and many had to accept different work.

The Carlisle Citizens' League was engaged in sending parcels to troops at the front and to those in prisoner of war (PoW) camps in Germany. Individual clubs organised collections, among them the Cumberland Motor Cycle Club who undertook a 'shilling collection' to provide Christmas treats for dispatch riders at the front. The papers continued to report what the various battalions of the Borders were doing in their training camps across the country, and in the case of 4 Border, in India. Recruitment widened with Carlisle taking men for both the Royal Naval Division, and Tyneside Irish, but numbers remained small.

The December meeting of the City Council debated a motion, which was presented annually, asking that meetings of the council should take place in the evenings to allow more working men to be able to stand for election. Time off was not given to attend council and other meetings so the representation of the working population was limited. As usual it was defeated.

War impinged more closely to home in the middle of December as the German navy shelled towns along the east coast of England, hitting Scarborough, Whitby and Hartlepool. Eighty-two people were reported killed and 250 injured. The papers were loud in condemning the German action adding this to the list of German atrocities cited as they advanced through Belgium and into France earlier in the year. Some from Carlisle had relatives in the towns and heard the news first hand later.

A positive response to the war was the opening in mid-December of the Union Jack Club in London Road. Intended for use by the wives of soldiers and sailors and other women, there was a restaurant, reading room and rest room, with a space for children to play railed off for safety.

By mid-December about 150 Belgians were in the city and the various committees and individuals put plans into action to give them a good Christmas. Hetherington Auctions for the first time charged for the catalogue for their horse sales; six boy scouts were engaged to sell them and all the funds were passed to the Belgian Refugee Fund. At an auction at Harrison's Mart in Carlisle a sheep was offered for sale, and then re-entered to be sold a further nine times. It raised a total of £29 2shillings (£2,500 in 2013).

Patrick Gormley, a successful cattle dealer, donated a bullock which was butchered by John Simpson, whose shop was in Lowther Street. Each of the refugees living in individual houses in the city received about 4lbs of meat, the remainder being sent to Rickerby Mansion and other houses where numbers of Belgians were housed. Plum puddings and mince pies had been sent to Rickerby and toys given by individuals and school groups arrived for distribution to the children. Father Knuckey arranged a special Christmas Mass at SS Mary and Joseph for the Belgians.

Lonsdales at the racecourse. Mike Milbourn

Lonsdale recruits at the racecourse, November 1914. Mike Milbourn

Christmas was celebrated at the racecourse headquarters of the 11 Border (Lonsdale) Battalion. Presents had arrived from Lady Valda Machell, wife of the commanding officer, in the form of 1,200 pairs of woollen mittens. Mrs Trench gave every man a copy of the Active Service Bible while Lord Lonsdale sent a pipe and tobacco pouch. He also sent 1,600lbs of plum pudding and 1,300 cigars to be added to the 1,000 cigars from another donor.

Other traditional events were held in the city. The annual Vynne-Lattimer dinner for the aged and poor was held in the dining room of the Great Central Hotel. These dinners had been started in about 1874 by Mr Vynne, a Norfolk man who moved to live and work in the city, and after his death in 1881 the tradition was continued by Mr Lattimer. Mr James Wheatley, a goldsmith, presided over the occasion which was attended by 180 people. A number of the city notables such as the Dalton family, the Wheatley family, the family of Dr Burn and the Stamper family from Dalston, all helped to serve the dinner of roast beef, pease pudding, potatoes, vegetables followed by plum pudding. The Reeves tea, held on Christmas Day at the Charlotte Street School involved a large number of local families as 'tea tray ladies and gentlemen'. A short concert was provided afterwards and presents were distributed; tea for the ladies and tobacco for the men.

In the New Year the City Education Committee received the annual report on the employment of 327 boys and 277 girls who had left school. Hudson Scott and Carr's were the main employers but other jobs were taken as messenger boys and porters, clerks, sawmill labourers, carpet makers and shop assistants.

A summary of trade in 1914 painted a gloomy picture. Cotton was particularly badly hit but Holme Head works had not suffered as badly as companies in other parts of the country. In contrast the woollen manufacturers had benefitted from the war. The Shaddon works, was making khaki yarn from 6am until 8pm. Waddels at Warwick Bridge had suffered a drop in orders at the beginning of the war but its fortunes were revived by an army order for blankets and another from the Lonsdale Battalion for a large quantity of hodden grey tweed for its

Lonsdale marching song, first performed at the racecourse 5 February 1915, refers to 'hodden grey' uniform. Mike Milbourn

uniforms. This specific mix of black and white wool yarn is referred to in *The Border Marching Song*, written for the Lonsdale Battalion.

Building work suffered with the outbreak of war but the new Post Office was nearly completed and a new school in Newtown kept a number of companies in work. Demand for timber to build huts at the Castle and for the Lonsdale Battalion at the racecourse had brought good trade to Creighton's timber yard.

By the end of 1914 Carlisle was gearing up for war. Meetings to plan support were increasingly well supported and large crowds gathered to cheer troops leaving the city. Community leaders, like the mayor and council, local bishops, clergy and ministers of all denominations and leading businessmen took responsibility for organising the city's response to events and other demands placed upon it. Many must have been at meetings on most evenings of the week.

The Castle, as the headquarters of the Border Regiment, was dealing with the recruitment and deployment of volunteers to Border battalions or other regiments and branches of the service. The racecourse had become the home and training ground of 11 Border (Lonsdale) Battalion; the Citadel station staff, Red Cross and VAD were becoming used to dealing with soldiers arriving and departing, whether individually on troop trains, or on trains carrying wounded men. Local hospitals were ready to accept casualties; businesses were gearing up for war production. Individuals had joined the League or one of the many other organisations to help and support soldiers, their wives, refugees and other citizens who were experiencing difficulties. Temperance was a live issue, as was poverty, housing and health.

CHAPTER 4

1915: War Comes to Carlisle

Lonsdales at the racecourse – Athletes Volunteer Force – Sport – Letters from the front – Rising food prices – Rolls of Honour – Slow down in recruitment – Charities and the Citizens' League – Crime, child neglect and morals – Fear of German attack – Entertainment – Police – Hospital trains – Discovering how to make dyes – School examinations – Early effect of the munitions works at Gretna – Relations with the farming community – GP services – Quintinshill rail disaster – The Whitsun Hiring – Munitions manufacture in Carlisle – Volunteers or conscripts? – Quintinshill Inquest – Buying materials of war – National Registration – Diseased cattle controversy – Shirkers – Building of Gretna – Entertainment and the young – Employment issues and tribunals – Control of drinking – Derby scheme and agricultural wages – Belgians in Carlisle – Christmas and New Year

Men arrived from France, or training in England, spent a few days at home and then returned. Hospital trains stopped for a few minutes in Citadel Station where the soldiers were given refreshments by members of the Red Cross or Voluntary Aid Detachment. The Citizens' League met weekly to co-ordinate the efforts of individuals and groups to support the war. Businesses looked forward with increasing confidence as orders from the War Office suggested that trade would be increased and sustained by the conflict.

Meanwhile 2 Border was recovering from its actions in France. The information from *Soldiers Died in the Great War* gives an incomplete picture but does in most cases include where a soldier, but not officers, were born, enlisted and lived at the time of their enlistment. The information concerning men from 2 Border killed in October 1914, was that of the 138 listed five came from Carlisle, with probably only one having close relatives in the city at the time of his death; a further seven originated from Cumberland. Although tragic and fully reported as losses from the local regiment, the actual effect on the people of the city might not be as great as the numbers suggest. However, losses from other regiments did bring tragedy to local families.

The Lonsdale Battalion continued to train at the racecourse and were often seen engaged in route marches, night exercises and rifle shooting on the range at Cummersdale. An appeal was published in the papers for the loan of small rifles and air rifles to teach those men who had never handled arms. The battalion undertook to return the items in a good and clean condition, but asked the owners to attach a small label to enable them to be identified. Recruiting improved and each week more men signed on at the Citizens' League.

Social events and concerts for the battalion were well organised, including a weekly concert in the Pavilion arranged by the YMCA. City notables, such as Theodore Carr, the Reverend Arthur Crosse, chaplain to the battalion, and his wife, attended and others including the Reverend May, Hermione Lediard, the 23-year-old daughter of Dr Lediard with her friend, 20-year-old Gwendoline Crosse played, sang, and took part in sketches accompanied by members of the battalion.

Drafts were sent from the Castle to join other battalions of the Border Regiment but with volunteers arriving regularly the number of men seen round the city wearing the red jacket of the volunteers did not drop below about 250. Other men preferred to join the Royal Naval Division, about 200 leaving to join their new companions at Crystal Palace in London. Private Peter Atkinson a 29-year-old former wool stapler of Junction Street, who was in the Argyll and Sutherland Highlanders, had leave in Carlisle. His personal recruitment campaign encouraged sixty-three men to join his regiment. He was given the recruiting bounty for each one and an extra week of leave to find more. Sadly, Sergeant Peter Atkinson was killed on 12 April 1918 and forty-three other men of the regiment who enlisted in Carlisle also died during the war.

Some men who, because of age or medical problems could not join the colours, enlisted in the Athletes Volunteer Force. Various groups were established in towns around both counties and a meeting in January 1915 concluded that some form of co-ordination was necessary if they were to train for the task of defending the country in the event of an invasion. The Central Association Volunteer Training Corps had been set up to serve as an umbrella for such ad hoc assemblies. The Carlisle group of about 120 men attended every Wednesday evening for drill in the Market Hall, and there were opportunities for small arms practice in Peter Street Hall.

The Football Association, in a decision criticised by many, decided to continue with fixtures and competitions. The first round of the English Cup saw Swansea defeat Blackburn, the match between Newcastle United and West Ham was drawn. Sunderland, South Shields and Darlington were all knocked out.

Many rugby clubs decided not to play league matches but a friendly was played between Carlisle and the Yeomanry who were training in the city. The match, in aid of local relief funds, attracted only a small crowd and was rather one-sided. Carlisle were the victors at 37–0 , and they played the match with only fourteen men. The press reported sporting fixtures rather further away. At Maymyo, Burma, H Company beat the rest of 4 Border in a cricket match by 52 runs, H Company scoring 161 with Private W.S. Clark as top scorer with 40. Closer to home the Lonsdale Battalion played Aspatria Athletic.

Fishing continued on the Eden and other rivers, although at the annual meeting of the Carlisle Angling Association there was concern at the drop in income because fewer people were buying visitor tickets. Carlisle and district dog owners were successful in the National Dog Show held in Birmingham. A report in February brought the happy news that after two days' absence, Winkles, the fox mascot of 5 Border, had returned to base in France unharmed. His final fate was never reported in the local press so whether he survived the war is unknown.

Letters home from soldiers were used to give sometimes very graphic details of actions and attacks which made very clear the dangers faced by loved ones at the front. Reports of action in more formal terms were reproduced either from official sources or national newspapers. A stoker who served on HMS *Tiger* returned to the city in February and while visiting his old school in Upperby, told the pupils how he was allowed on deck to see the *Blücher* sink during the Battle of Dogger Bank.

The price of foodstuffs continued to rise during the early part of 1915, to the extent that some began to suggest that the government should take control of supplies; this was met with opposition both by local businessmen and the press. The *Journal* quoted an article in *The Times* of the scene in London docks where:

> *'The abundance of the good things which are being poured into the lap of the docks reaches almost fabulous proportions. There has been nothing like it since London became a port. The port granaries contain about 2,000 tons of wheat in ordinary times. Today they hold ten or twelve times that amount. Sugar usually runs to about 20,000 tons. The year's supply bought by the Government is now being brought into port with the result that the quantity in the warehouses amounts to an unprecedented figure of 80,000 tons. The correspondent says, "it is like starving in a land of plenty".'*

A number of possible culprits were suggested as being likely to gain by the increase in price, notably the flour millers and others involved in the processing and selling of food. The prices continued to rise during the month and in just one week the cost of a stone of flour in Carlisle went up by 3d to 2s 8d. This of course led to a rise in the cost of bread and other food staples.

The Old Boys of Carlisle Grammar School, the Old Carliols' Club, at their annual meeting had to elect new officials to replace those who had gone to join the war. One member of the Old Carliols' Club, George Routledge, completed a register of Carliols by adding the names and units of those old boys who were serving in the conflict.

It was agreed that members in the services would be excused from paying their annual subscriptions. The committee of the Cumberland Motor Cycle Club similarly decided to make all those who had joined the war honorary members for the duration.

Recording the names of those from churches, schools and clubs who had joined the services was undertaken by most such organisations.

Businesses in the city published in the papers lists of their men who had joined the colours, and churches often had similar lists in the porch. Ten of the Carr's Athletic Club team who played in the Carlisle Charity Shield in 1914 were in the army by February 1915.

Recruiting remained slow; throughout January an average of only about thirty men a day were presenting themselves at the Castle and the newly-built huts on the adjoining land which could accommodate 1,000 men were empty. Meetings were planned with well-known speakers to encourage young men to do their duty. The men who had volunteered and completed their basic training left the Castle in groups accompanied to the station by a local band, usually that of Caldew Vale but also from the RAOB and St Andrew's, which took a turn at cheering the men on their way to the battalion depots at Shoeburyness or Southend.

The Citizens' League organised the making, collection and distribution of clothing to soldiers. Those who could afford to buy gifts for distribution to wounded and sick soldiers in the hospitals gave more personal gifts of food, cigarettes, chocolate and fruit. Charity collections of a different order exercised Canon Rawnsley. He wrote to the *Journal* in January 1915 asking readers to contribute to a fund for mobile canteens to provide men arriving or departing from bases in France with hot drinks and food. At a meeting in his capacity as a member of the county education committee the canon suggested that it should be possible for the children of the city and county to make wooden toys in school woodwork lessons to replace those previously imported from Germany.

Pre-existing charities were concerned that the war would make such calls on people's generosity that funds they needed to continue working would be squeezed. The National Union of Railwaymen's charity supported 1,849 orphans in all parts of the country and held a concert and collection to maintain its funds. In addition to the ticket money the paper listed contributions to the funds from individuals, Mr Buck, Mr Chance, Mr Hepworth and Sir Benjamin Scott sent 10s each; George White, Theodore Carr and Bertram Carr each sent 5s.

The scouts carried out an increasing range of jobs within the city acting as messengers, as police observers guarding parts of the railway, giving out refreshments to troops on trains passing through the station and supporting the work of the Citizens' League. The organisation was suffering from a lack of leaders and instructors as many of them had joined the army and in January George Saul wrote to the papers asking for people to volunteer as scoutmasters and to instruct in military pioneering.

Unpleasant aspects of life continued in the city. Cases of child neglect were investigated by the National Society for the Prevention of Cruelty to Children (NSPCC). The juvenile court dealt with a range of offences. On a typical day in late February the court considered a case of the theft of builders' equipment, one boy was sentenced to six strokes of the birch, another fined 10s (50p). Two boys aged eight and ten had previously appeared before the court and were given four strokes of the birch.

Four boys aged seven and eight were caught having a stone fight in Warwick Road, pulling up the tarmac to get the stones. Eight boys were fined for selling newspapers without a licence. In another case a gang of boys were accused of two offences, breaking into a school and causing damage, for which they were fined 1s and their parents had to pay to repair the display cases they had broken. Their other offence was breaking into Carr's factory and stealing biscuits.

Morals, particularly those of women, were the concern of the Council for Rescue and Prevention Work in Cumberland and Westmorland. Their intention was 'to set before girls the noblest ideals of life and marriage and encourage mothers to accept and fulfil their home responsibilities'. Established in 1914 the first annual meeting was held in Carlisle, chaired by the Bishop of Barrow and attended, among others, by Canon Rawnsley, Mr de Schmid, the Chief Constable, Miss Matravers and Miss Henderson. Much of the work involved getting young women to join the League of Honour through clubs and classes but there was difficulty in getting people in some areas to accept that there were moral issues to be addressed. In an attempt to widen the role of the organisation Canon Rawnsley referred to the work of women police who patrolled New York to deal with issues of morals which male officers found difficult. St Mary's Home for Penitents on Myddleton Street in Carlisle already gave shelter to those who were 'rescued'. As with other charitable organisations the work needed funding. The first year's work had been paid for by donations from fifty individuals and the parishioners of Stanwix.

The naval attacks on the east coast, the increasing Zeppelin activity and German advances in France led to some concern that the Germans might appear on the west coast. Police and military met together to discuss action to be taken if there was an invasion. Although the risk was thought to be small the need for police and military to co-operate and the role of the volunteer forces were all discussed. There was agreement that if there was an invasion all public houses would be closed immediately.

Recruiting continued to be slow as the *Journal* reported in a typical paragraph:

> *'Recruitment for all the local units of the army has become very quiet and although men continue to arrive at the Castle it cannot be claimed that Carlisle or north Cumberland is helping to swell the ranks of recruits at the present time.'*

Ten men went to Kendal to join 4 Border and in the preceding weeks ninety men went to the racecourse to join the Lonsdales. Some in Carlisle, while arguing to protect businesses which needed to retain skilled men, expressed the view that certain farmers were using unfair and dubious methods to protect their labour, particularly their sons. Farmers countered with the argument that they were equally in need

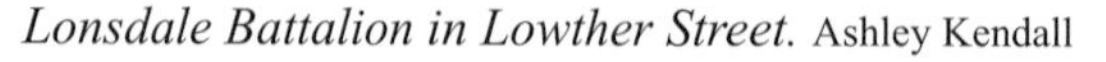
Lonsdale Battalion in Lowther Street. Ashley Kendall

Blackwell Racecourse, first home of the Lonsdales. Denis Perriam

of skilled labour and it was not possible to replace men who over their lifetime had farming bred into them with others from a background in towns, or without the knowledge to carry out the tasks.

The Lonsdales were seen regularly, marching, carrying out company or battalion exercises and practising musketry. Equipment continued to arrive and the men were getting used to marching carrying their full packs. A march through the city by the whole battalion caused great excitement:

> *'The long procession of over 1,200 men of splendid physique was a matter of great interest to the citizens who happened to be in the streets at the time and many flattering comments were made on the men's appearance.'*

Lady Lonsdale issued an appeal for musical instruments for the battalion in the local press. A new washroom had been opened giving more men the opportunity to wash in hot water in the morning. Also a drying room was being prepared to dry out greatcoats after the night exercises and marches.

Leisure activities were changing. The Carlisle Music Festival was cancelled for the duration of the war but was replaced by smaller competitions, like one set up for business girls. Sidney Bacon, sold his interest in Her Majesty's Theatre to a London company. His reason was not financial as returns were good, but he was changing his business from theatres to picture houses.

The Home Food Culture Movement set up a branch in the city in mid-August 1914. The rise in prices of food encouraged people to try to grow food of their own. There were already some allotments in the city and the Home Culture Committee identified land which could be brought into cultivation. New allotments were set up in Cargo, at Greystone Road and the boys of the Grammar School cultivated a model plot on the Warwick Road.

The outbreak of war put a great strain on the police, particularly as they were at first responsible for guarding Carlisle's many rail lines, junctions and sidings. As things became more organised the weekly leave day was reinstated and men who had lost annual leave were given time off. In common with other employers the police had lost members to the army, five Reservists were recalled and others had volunteered. The force carried out collections for the local relief fund and gathered clothes and other items to send to their colleagues in the army.

The Chief Constable also oversaw the work of the fire service and ambulance. The worst fire of the year was that at Sundour textiles which did damage to the value of £30,000 (over £2million now). In addition there had been thirty other fires and the horse ambulance had responded to seventy calls to accidents or to transport people to hospital. In comparison there were 10,500 calls for ambulance assistance alone within the city in 2012-13.

The City Education Committee had taken over responsibility for children's education from the county in the previous year and was keen to get some projects underway, particularly the provision of a technical school and a new open-air school. For many years there had been attempts to get a technical school opened in the city but the County

Council had refused, even when pressured by the Board of Education in London.

The council had to deal with the upkeep of the city's streets. Scotland Road was described as being like a ploughed field, the state of the tramways, particularly the one crossing the Eden Bridge, led to many complaints by those doused in cold and muddy water by passing vehicles. Many of the roads were constructed from granite setts, hard wearing but noisy and prone to become dislodged. Tarmacadam was the popular replacement, but was only used in a few repairs because of the expense. Letters in the paper complained of the dangers to the public caused by the poor quality of setts in Botchergate, and a large puddle in the lane between Gloucester Road and Hasell Street which forced pedestrians to risk either a soaking, or being injured by squeezing past the thorn bushes which lined the lane.

Rain and cold also had a bad effect on the troops in France. A large number of men were on the sick and injured list sent to the Castle in early February, many were wounded but a large number were suffering from rheumatism, rheumatic fever, frostbite and pneumonia. Families reading this sent items such as rubber boots, coats and knitted clothing. The papers carried advertisements extolling the virtues of additional equipment to send to men in France.

Companies were quick to advertise comforts to be sent to the troops. Cumbrian Newspapers Ltd

Telegrams: "Rubber," Carlisle.

ARMY EQUIPMENT

WOLSLEY VALISES,
CAMP SHEETS, BUCKETS,
BASINS, AIR PILLOWS.

Quick Dispatch.

CARLISLE RUBBER CO.,
87, Lowther Street, Carlisle.

Telephone: 118, Carlisle.

The hospital trains continued to stop at the station on their way to Glasgow, Aberdeen or Perth. The Red Cross, VAD and scouts distributed the gifts donated by the Carlisle people. The possibility that a train would one day stop to deliver patients to the hospital in the city seemed to be coming closer when officers from the army visited the Cumberland Infirmary, the Chadwick School and Murrell Hill House to check that they were ready to receive men. The Citizens' League set up sub-committees, one for each of the hospitals, to co-ordinate support from the community.

The risk of air raids led to the imposition of lighting regulations which required shopkeepers to turn off bright signs, and for streets with many lights to have some turned off to break up the pattern when seen from the air. Factories with glass roofs had to put up shading to block lights at night, all lights had to be reduced to a minimum including trams where it was just possible for the conductor to see to issue tickets. The population was told how they were supposed to behave if there was an air raid. The police would give warning of a raid by ringing handbells and once the signal had sounded people should take refuge in their houses, using cellars and basements if they had them.

A particularly violent and sudden storm hit the area on 18 March. The wind accompanied by snow brought blizzard conditions into the Solway, where the fishing fleet from Annan was working. Many boats managed to run for shelter but three of the seventeen were lost with their crews. Two railway workers were killed near Hawick when they apparently failed to hear the approach of the delayed express from Edinburgh. City roads were blocked by snow and slush; nothing of the sort had been experienced so late in the year since records began in 1798. Trains into the city from all directions were delayed or had to wait until conditions improved.

The Lonsdales got closer to moving away. Placed into the Fifth Army, 37th Division, 112 Brigade, the men were inspected by the Chief Medical Inspector who described them as the 'finest men he had seen anywhere'. Canon Hicks, from Lincoln, arrived to talk to the men about the YMCA and what it did for the troops in France. The battalion supported a concert enjoyed by 450 men and officers. Major Binning thanked the people of Carlisle for their many kindnesses to the battalion during their stay at the racecourse; the work of the YMCA was particularly appreciated notably in setting up and encouraging the regular concerts and sports events.

Lonsdale sports at the racecourse. Mike Milbourn

A major breakthrough by the chemists at Morton Sundour saved the industries of the city dependent on dyes. Once the German source of dyes had been cut off the British Government decided that it would allow companies to see the patents of German firms. Beginning work in late 1914 Morton Sundour chemists produced the first colours, blue and yellow and made them available in commercial quantities by March 1915. It was not without some cost to the city as the process involved the heating of oil derived from coal tar which made the works sited near to houses very unpopular until they developed a more efficient process.

The first trainload of wounded to be admitted to the hospitals in Carlisle arrived on 22 March. One hundred men, all of whom were capable of sitting and walking, were sent from Southampton. Sadly the arrangements to greet the men and get them to hospital were not well organised. Men were brought off the train in ones and twos without considering that they were going to different destinations so had to be sorted on the station concourse. Although the date and time of the train's arrival had supposedly been kept secret, a large crowd gathered on the viaduct and it took the combined efforts of the police and some men of the Lonsdale Battalion to keep a clear route for the cars.

Some of the cars had so many civilian passengers who had come to greet the train there was only room for one or two soldiers. The papers reported that in some instances three civilians were sitting in the body of the car and two soldiers were perched on the small 'dickey' seat at the rear. This was bad enough if the men were reasonably uninjured, but one soldier was seen with one arm in plaster and a sling, his greatcoat over the other arm, trying to avoid being thrown from his perch at the rear of a car as it bounced off past the Citadel. Food and drink had been provided but when the last soldier eventually departed it was discovered that they, along with the blankets and wraps which had been provided by the Citizens' League, were still piled up on trolleys waiting to be used.

A letter from the County Director of VAD in Cumberland in the press on 30 March replied to the criticisms levelled at the organisation. The men, he said, had not been removed from the train in batches to go to the same hospital because the assessment of their needs was only done once they had disembarked. The greater efficiency with which subsequent trains were unloaded and the men dealt with indicated that lessons were learned as the local VAD came to grips with the problems.

A joint meeting of the Education Committees of Carlisle and Cumberland, with head teachers and governors was held towards the end of March. The topics under discussion were the Board of Education scheme for examinations; the age of leaving secondary school; the standardisation of school reports and; the relation between the curricula of primary and secondary schools. Miss Frances Bevan, Head of Carlisle Girls' Grammar School said that in her opinion the board wished to control, by means of the university examination bodies, all school examinations in those schools receiving its grant. The board's action would result in it having direct control of the school curriculum; this was not popular among those at the meeting who wished to retain more local control.

Discussion on the length of school life focused on the cost, not to the school system but to parents, of maintaining children without earning for more than the present four years. There was a conflict between elementary schools wanting to keep children until fourteen, and secondary schools wanting them at the age of twelve. Debates on education would intensify as the war progressed.

The Lonsdale Battalion held what was thought would be its final parade at the racecourse on 1 April 1915. There were a number of leaving parties in the city and the employees of Hudson Scott held a whist drive and social for former colleagues and their wives. Their departure was delayed and it wasn't until 3 May that an advanced party left for Prees Heath in Staffordshire.

As the pace of the war quickened Sir John French complained on 27 March that battles had been nearly lost because of a lack of ammunition. In the face of increasing press criticism the government took action and even before Lloyd George was appointed Minister of Munitions in May 1915 work began to increase the supply. Engineering companies were asked to manufacture shells and new factories were built. A 'new government factory' was planned to be built 'somewhere on the Scottish border'. Although ten miles from the city, the secret munitions works at Gretna and Longtown was to have a huge effect on Carlisle.

It was during the early months of 1915 that surveyors began work on the mosslands on the banks of the Solway to lay out the working areas, rail lines and other buildings which would make up the factory, nine miles long by three miles wide. Although secret, the activities at the sites were sometimes reported but without identifying the location. What was reported were the incidents of drunkenness among the labour force building the factory, the difficulty of getting sufficient accommodation in the city, the only settlement of any size near the works, and the attraction of the pay which, as the site grew, made competition for workers even more difficult for Carlisle employers.

Often the first indication the public had of an action in France was when the casualty lists were published and the letters informing relatives of the death, injury or unknown whereabouts of their loved ones began to drop through the letter box. The *Journal* of 16 April published a list of nearly sixty men of 2 Border who had been killed at the Battle of Neuve Chapelle which took place between 10 and 13 March. The list was published on 27 March and the later records show that ninety-five men died between 10 and 27 March of which one was listed as living in Carlisle and four as having been born in the city. Many of the recruits to the regiment came from other parts of the country; while six of those killed had been recruited in Carlisle, twenty-one had signed on in Manchester.

It wasn't just men from the district who were in danger; 22-year-old Catharine Marguerite Beauchamp Waddell, known as Beauchamp, was serving with the First-Aid Nursing Yeomanry Corps (FANY) in France. Her family came from Wetheral and in April she wrote to friends about her adventures working in a hospital which adjoined the cathedral in Calais. On 18 March she was arrested as a spy, but gave no details apart from the fact that she had just avoided being locked up in the citadel prison. On the following day she was left in charge of the ward while the sister went for dinner. Thinking a 'whirring noise' was the plane of an airman flying over who had been to tea the previous day, she went outside and realised it was a Zeppelin. She rushed back into the ward to calm delirious patients and ensure that all were safe while guns blazed away all round the town.

After apparently moving away the airship returned and dropped a bomb which broke all the hospital windows and damaged the cathedral, debris from the roof and a falling wall covered the patients and staff with dust and pelted them with bricks. They were saved from greater damage by a buttress which diverted the falling wall away from them.

The Mayor officiated at the opening of the extended electricity works which dated from 1899 but changes in technology and the growth in population required that improvements be made. The supply and the cost of making and distributing both gas and electricity were recurring problems for the council.

The increasing demand for men to join the army resulted in employers being asked whether some jobs could be taken by women. Not all employers and certainly not the unions were initially in favour of the leap into the unknown. The reports acknowledged that training replacement workers would prove a temporary inconvenience but that maintaining the output of industry was vital. The lists of men leaving firms were published and the loss of police officers and council workers was reported through meetings of the city council.

Members of the National Union of Women Workers attended a lecture by Mrs Chance of Morton on temperance. The topic of drinking and the effects of alcohol was becoming an increasingly contentious issue with many calls for restricting if not banning the sale of alcohol. The advocates of limitation all mentioned the effect of missed days at work, of the inefficiency of soldiers in training and the consequences of treating drinks, including incidents of soldiers the worse for drink falling out of trains and being killed. At the same meeting another speaker told of the work of the union in helping to address the problem of immorality among women and young girls. The work of women patrols was alluded to and described as being very effective in getting girls to take up useful work.

Some employers, especially farmers who were accused of trying to shield their sons, were accused of not releasing staff but manipulating the number of employees and, in the case of farmers, the jobs their sons were given. The demand for full conscription to replace of dependence on volunteers grew during the spring of 1915. Complaints that some were avoiding the moral call to arms were denied but it was clear that there were not enough men coming forward to replace the mounting casualties. Firms, like the railway companies, Carr's and Hudson Scott still retained a number of men of military age. Their argument was that these men were essential to sustain the business and the authorities were unable to challenge this position.

Efforts were made in all parts of the city, and more widely across the county, to encourage recruitment but the numbers coming forward continued to fall. At the end of April the recruiting office for the district moved from the Castle to that of the Citizens' League in Devonshire Street. Men continued to arrive at the Castle, but they were from the Manchester offices which were getting recruits for the Border Regiment. These men were accommodated in the barracks and began their basic training.

Two hundred and eight men of the 4 Border who had elected for home service moved from their base in Blackpool on 28 April. They arrived in Carlisle and, once the leaks in the roof had been repaired, were put into billets with their HQ established at the Drill Hall in Strand Road. Training continued at The Swifts with route marches around the city. Others of the battalion who were tasked with home defence were sent to Barrow. The city took on an increasingly military look with the Border recruits, the 4th and 11th Battalions and the Cumberland and Westmorland Yeomanry all based in and around Carlisle.

The increasing demand for medical officers put pressure on the local

Yeomanry sports day. Ashley Kendall

GPs to consider ways of reorganising their services. They met and agreed that they would arrange to keep the practices of those who went to the army, and provide a medical service for troops in the city. To supplement the income of the men joining the RAMC domestic fees and expenses charged to patients were to be shared. The doctor providing the cover would take five eighths in a town and three quarters in a country practice. Tuberculosis patients would be shared among the remaining doctors.

On 22 April the Cumberland and Westmorland Antiquarian Society met in Carlisle. A visit to the cathedral formed part of the meeting and members were shown masonry which had been buried to form gun platforms last used in the English Civil War. Members had been carrying out research into a number of topics and there were descriptions of an archaeological excavation at Newbiggin Hall which discovered the old entrance to the tower. Another speaker told of excavations at a supposed Roman camp near Alston. The excavation of the Roman camp at Ambleside would be continued in August as sufficient funds had been collected to finance the work.

The price of spirits was increased at the beginning of May. A new tax led to a 2s (£6.50 in 2013) increase in the price of a bottle of whisky. A small glass went up by 1d and a whole glass by 2d. There were similar increases in the price of brandy and rum. Not all publicans raised their prices on the same day. This caused disagreement at the next meeting of the Licensed Victuallers Association when those who had kept prices down were accused of trading unfairly. The reason they gave was that they had stock put by and only raised the prices when they replenished their cellars.

The landings on the Dardanelles took place on 25 April and involved men of 1 Border. Alexander Cornock was the only man killed who was listed as a Carlisle resident and James Cavill had been born in the city and enlisted at the Castle. A further six had enlisted at

The Lonsdales leave Carlisle for Prees Heath Staffordshire. Mike Milbourn

Lonsdales at Citadel Station. Mike Milbourn

Carlisle, most from other parts of Cumberland. The majority had little connection to the city and county, although the commanding officer Colonel Hume who fell with his men was well known as he had spent time as commanding officer at the Castle between 1909 and 1912 when he and his wife, Juliana, lodged at 80 Warwick Road. One of the wounded officers, Captain Harrison, was born in Carlisle and had attended school here as well as holding the position of adjutant to the special reserve at the Castle. On 3 May the Lonsdales finally left for Staffordshire.

The press were keen to publish news of men serving abroad and encouraged families to send extracts from letters they received. In the edition of the *Journal* of 7 May 1915 the paper included stories headed: 'CARLISLE MAN ON BOARD A TRANSPORT' which told of Percy Hayton, whose family lived at 6 Hart Street, unloading a troopship in the Mediterranean. Sidney Dixon's parents in Regent Street sent in his account of the trenches which was headlined, 'CARLISLE MAN WITH THE CANADIANS'; a man serving with the Canadian medical corps wrote of '1,200 PATIENTS IN 24 HOURS'. The son of a Keswick Methodist minister told of 'THE CANADIAN'S GALLANTRY. 'GREYSTOKE MAN IN A RAIN OF SHELLS' was self-explanatory, as was 'DALSTON MOTOR DRIVER UNDER SHELL FIRE'; and 'KESWICK MAN ON HILL 60'.

Another man wrote to describe *'French women and agricultural work'* in which he mentioned that the farm work was being done by old men and women as all the young men were in the army. Other stories told of 'A WHITEHAVEN MAN IMPRISONED IN GERMANY', 'A LANGHOLM MAN'S BAPTISM OF FIRE'; 'SHELLED RIGHT AND LEFT'; and 'BARRACK LIFE IN POONA'.

The sinking of the RMS *Lusitania* on 7 May on a voyage from New York to Liverpool not only shocked America and was instrumental in changing public opinion there to consider entering the war, but also encouraged a rise in the number of men in England, including Carlisle, volunteering to fight. Stories of atrocities were often included in the Carlisle papers, taken from reports in the national press to show what the enemy was capable of doing to civilians and captured soldiers.

A disaster closer to home on Saturday, 22 May had a great effect on life in the city. It involved eight railwaymen who lived in Etterby and Carlisle and worked engines from the Caledonian Railway Company depot at Kingmoor. It was caused by a coincidence of events including the SS *Aquitania* running aground at Liverpool, the increase in traffic because of the war which resulted in trains running late, and a signalman saving himself a mile-long walk to work at Quintinshill, near Gretna.

At Quintinshill the signal box controlled the track between the boxes at Gretna to the south and Kirkpatrick Fleming to the north, there were also two loop lines to allow trains to wait as faster traffic passed. On this morning two northbound expresses, scheduled to leave Carlisle at 5.50am and 6.05am, were both running late and a goods train which left the Kingmoor depot north of the city at 5.50am going in the same direction was an hour behind schedule. A local passenger train going north out of Carlisle on time at 6.10am was going to have to be stopped somewhere to allow the expresses to pass.

A troop train carrying about 500 men of the 7th Battalion, Royal Scots Regiment left Larbert, north of Edinburgh, about 4.30am heading south for Liverpool. The train was made up of fifteen ageing wooden-framed carriages, borrowed from the Great Central Railway, with five luggage vans and a guards van attached behind. The men should have travelled to Liverpool on the previous Wednesday but the grounding of the SS *Aquitania* delayed their departure. Even on this trip the train was behind its planned schedule.

Instead of changing shifts at 6am the signal men in the box near Quintinshill had a long-standing agreement to have a late handover to allow the relief man to ride the local passenger train from its scheduled stop at Gretna station, thereby saving a walk. At Quintinshill there were the two main lines and also two 'loops', stretches of track where trains could be moved off the mainline to wait without blocking traffic. The Kingmoor Depot was full so George Meakin, the night duty signalman, moved an empty southbound coal train onto the southbound loop to wait. The late running goods from Carlisle got to the box at 6.14am and was placed on the northbound loop. The northbound passenger train arrived slightly early bringing James Tinsley, his relief, and was standing outside the box, having crossed onto the southbound line to let the expresses through.

Tinsley was trying to catch up on the paperwork as the first of the late northbound trains passed and he accepted the southbound troop train from Larbert into his section at 6.42am, apparently forgetting about the local train stationary on the southbound track. Important safety practices which should have alerted him had been overlooked and the scene was set for what remains to this day Britain's worst rail disaster.

At 6.46am the second northbound Glasgow express, pulled by two engines to get up Beattock Bank, passed Gretna and Tinsley accepted it into the Quintinshill section of track. Four minutes later the troop train, driven by Francis Scott and fired by James Hannah, at a speed later estimated to be about seventy miles per hour, approached and the crew of the local train saw it coming. The troop train crew, having seen the danger, managed to slow to about forty miles per hour before running head first into the local train; both Scott and Hannah died instantly. One engine rode up over the other and the coaches carrying the soldiers, many asleep, concertinaed and fell onto the northbound line, catching fire from the ruptured gas cylinders used for lighting.

John Cowper and Andrew Johnston tried to stop their northbound express when they saw the guard of the local train waving at them but it was too late and they ran into the local train's carriages before stopping suddenly when they hit the engine of the troop train across their tracks. Both the men in the leading engine were partly buried by coal which slipped forward from the tender, Cowper up to his neck, and they had to be dug out by the crew of the engine behind them. More than 200 died in the resulting inferno and a further 200 were injured. Some of these arrived in Carlisle with others taken to Scottish hospitals.

A sailor, thought to have been on the Glasgow express, somehow got a lift south and arrived at Carlisle central police station where he told the superintendent on duty about the crash; he didn't mention the fire. Eric de Schmid, Chief Constable and head of the rescue services, was telephoned at home by the police. He rang Citadel Station where a clerk told him that Mr Campbell, the Superintendent, had already left on a rescue train. Before leaving himself he rang the Red Cross and arranged for their volunteers to travel to the site.

De Schmid arrived at 10am and found the fire crew trying to run a hose from the Sark, a small river about half a mile from the crash. The survivors and local volunteers were trying to pull survivors and bodies out of the flaming wreckage. Word had got to the Citizens' League in Carlisle and more volunteers arrived, some with cars ready to carry the injured to hospital. Eleven Carlisle doctors and four nurses went to the site, with others arriving from nearby from Longtown and more from as far away as Penrith. There is an account of 30-year-old Dr Edwards, a surgeon at the infirmary, assisted by Dr Matthews, having to amputate a man's leg to release him from the wreckage while fire burned next to them. Survivors were unstinting in their praise of the bravery and dedication of the Carlisle doctors and nurses and the support from local people and others who drove or cycled from the city.

Crowds arrived at Quintinshill. Ashley Kendall

The first fifty-two casualties arrived in Carlisle by train at 10.42am, quickly followed by others at 11.12 and 11.51am. They were taken to Canal Station, on a siding near the Carr's biscuit works, which had been built by the railway companies to get injured to the Infirmary quickly in the event of a train crash. Here they were met by doctors and nurses and members of the Carr's Biscuit company fire brigade who helped carry the stretchers into the Infirmary. The others were sent to Murrell Hill House, Chadwick and Fusehill Hospitals, and also to The Viaduct Temperance Hotel, Great Central Hotel, County Hotel and Carlisle Castle.

The Citizens' League members played their part, Mr Johnston, who owned a tea and coffee merchants with a restaurant in English Street, drove to Gretna and used his car to carry bodies between the crash site and the temporary mortuary. George Wheatley, the confectioner from Botchergate, carried a supply of bandages to Gretna and his car was used as a mobile supply store. Other members took and distributed food and drinks at the site and in the hospitals. The Carlisle Red Cross had fifteen nurses at Quintinshill, and many of them travelled back with the injured in private cars and on the trains. Others remained in the city to help in the hospitals and homes. On the evening of the crash two hospital trains went through the station and the Brampton VAD distributed refreshments as usual.

As Sunday morning dawned the Carlisle fire brigade and Mr de Schmid were still at the scene trying to cool the wreckage to allow rescue workers search for bodies. The Citizens' League compiled the official list of those in Carlisle hospitals and those who had died in the city and assisted when relatives arrived. Work at the crash site continued all day involving men from the Caledonian yard at Kingmoor.

The fate of the Carlisle men on the engines was known by Sunday morning. Francis Scott had worked on the Caledonian Railway for many years and had the distinction of having driven trains carrying three monarchs, Queen Victoria, King Edward VII and most recently, just a week before the crash, the train taking King George V on a tour of Scottish munitions factories. He and his fireman attended the Etterby Mission Church where Scott was superintendent of the Sunday school; he was married with seven children and a grandchild all at home at 2 Etterby Road. James Hannah lived at 11 Scaurbank Road, less than a

An ambulance train collecting the injured at Quintinshill. Ashley Kendall

Quintinshill survivors at Chadwick Memorial Hospital awaiting the cortege of Driver Scott and Fireman Hannah. Mrs Donald is the Commandant, and 3 of the nurses are Miss Boyers, Miss Ferguson, Miss Robinson. Ashley Kendall

The funeral carriages of Frances Scott and James Hannah at the corner of Etterby Street. Ashley Kendall

Drivers and firemen of the Caledonian railway at the funeral following the cortege in Etterby Street. Ashley Kendall

mile from Scott. David Wallace who had been driving the local train was born in Motherwell but was living in Carlisle. Both he and his fireman, George Hutchinson, who had been lodging in the centre of Carlisle, were uninjured. Wallace returned to the scene on the Sunday morning to help with the recovery work.

The impact of the crash continued to reverberate round the city. On Tuesday, 25 May the inquest was opened and adjourned in Carlisle on the first twenty-one victims. The legal situation was confused as although the accident had occurred about a mile on the Scottish side of the border many of the victims had either died on their journey to Carlisle or in hospital in the city. Questioned by the Carlisle coroner, Thomas Slack Strong, signalman James Tinsley admitted he had forgotten about the local passenger train on the wrong line.

Next day the funerals were held of the two railway men. There was a large procession headed by one hundred railway men from the Caledonian company, followed by fifty children and teachers from the Etterby Mission Sunday School. The hearses came next, followed by carriages carrying the members of the men's families. The coffins were carried by colleagues of the two men, including some who had been involved in the crash. David Todhunter, fireman on the pilot engine and John Graham, who was firing the second engine on the Glasgow express, helped to carry James Hannah to his final rest in Stanwix Cemetery. The full inquest and inquiry followed later.

The war continued to impact on local labour and agriculture. Before the fair held in the previous autumn Canon Rawnsley had urged girls to encourage the men to sign up for the army. Farmers complained at the Whitsun fair that the number of men making themselves available was many fewer than in a normal year. The presence of recruiting sergeants at the fairs was thought to have put some off and worse, from the point of view of the farmers, succeeded in convincing others to join the colours. Farmers were worried that without sufficient men they would be unable to gather the harvest.

Some local companies were suffering shortages and the employment of women and volunteers was again suggested. The railway union was convinced that women could not be drivers, firemen and guards. Behind the argument was the fear that the railway companies would pay women at a lower rate than men, and thereby cut wages generally. The Citizens' League meeting on 13 June heard

Survivors of Quintinshill at City Hospital, Fusehill. Ashley Kendall

Dr Aitken outline a scheme for giving women first aid training. The Chief Constable, having resisted the idea for some time, asked the League to advertise for Special Constables, at first for duty on Sunday only.

Three weeks after the Quintinshill crash sixty-six soldiers were put on an ambulance train to move to hospital in Edinburgh. A large crowd gathered at the top of the ramp leading onto the viaduct and cheered the fifty-four men who could walk. The train then went to the Canal Station to pick up another twelve who were carried on stretchers. There remained seventy-seven casualties in hospitals, hotels and private houses.

The Hiring Fair recruitment drive was successful, fifty-five of the 272 volunteers had addresses in Carlisle. The Border Regiment took ninety-seven, a further thirty-nine joined the Lonsdale Battalion and 136 enlisted in a host of other regiments and services, including the South Wales Borderers' Bantams Battalion which enrolled five men from the city. News of life in the Lonsdale Battalion in their camp at

Quintinshill survivors and nurses at the Infirmary. Carlisle Library

Special Constables parade. Denis Perriam

Prees Heath, Staffordshire was reported in some detail. Promotions were listed and the officers and men who were going to other camps for specialist training were named. As the war progressed, the level of detail in these reports diminished.

Dr Beard had been instrumental in developing the children's nursery which provided day care for children whose mothers were ill or working. It moved to larger premises in Abbey Street because it was felt that with men going to war and women increasingly entering work the need would increase and the new location was more accessible.

Juvenile crime continued to be a problem with the monthly children's court hearing of cases of two boys' theft of cigarettes, one taking of money from family members and others taking and selling a bicycle; their parents were fined 10s. Another case involved the theft of a bicycle valued at 30s which was sold to a soldier of the Lonsdale Battalion for 2s. The soldier, who was also arrested, received a caution from the magistrate, Sir Benjamin Scott, and the admonition that 'boys would not steal bicycles if nobody bought them from them'. A number of boys were fined for breaking windows in the New Brewery in Shaddongate and others for the same offence in Thomas Street.

The care of soldiers in the Red Cross hospitals and the Infirmary was supported by gifts from many of the citizens. A letter in mid-June in the *Journal* complained that when the writer, who didn't give a name, arrived at the Castle to hand over some comforts for the men in hospital they had been refused. At the end of June an article explained that the men in the Castle were subject to War Office rules which did not allow for the receipt of presents. However the rules were being reviewed to bring their treatment into line with men in the other hospitals.

A later article complained that although the War Office had issued a circular easing visiting and other restrictions, the situation at the Castle had not improved. For some reason the men in the hospital there were still not allowed to receive presents which those in auxiliary hospitals were getting regularly. Attempts to give food, fruit and flowers had been refused and offers of car rides declined. The people of the city became increasingly frustrated and angry at the perceived unfairness.

In contrast to the treatment of these men there were reports in the same edition of patients from the Chadwick Memorial Hospital being taken out for tea at Kirkandrews, another group went to Stanwix tennis club and on another day Mr and Mrs Chance provided their car to take men to Quarry Hill. The men from Murrell Hill House were taken by car to Talkin Tarn by Miss Edith Breton, of Aglionby Street, a teacher at the Girls' High School, and Miss Elise Sprott, a clerk who lived in Lonsdale Street. The manager of Her Majesty's Theatre invited the men to see the Saturday afternoon performance.

The new Minister of Munitions, Lloyd George, made a speech in Manchester which was extensively reported in Carlisle. In it he appealed for manufacturers and workers to co-operate in making sufficient munitions to protect those men who had volunteered to join the army and serve. He said 'we were the worst organised nation in the world for this war'.

Carlisle was ahead of the minister. On 9 June, two weeks before Lloyd George's speech, the local MP, Richard Denman, called a meeting at his house, St Nicholas View, to explore how Carlisle could make a greater contribution to munitions manufacture. Theodore Carr, of the biscuit factory, was elected as a neutral but effective chairman of a committee made up of local engineering businesses and trades unions, including Hudson Scott; Cowans Sheldon; Pratchitts; Angus Sanderson; the County Garage, James Fendley, motor engineer and Tyer and Co. There was also representation from the Amalgamated Society of Engineers; the Steam Engine Makers' Society; the National Union of Gas Workers and Labourers and the Iron Founders Association. The secretary to the committee was Henry Campbell, a stock and insurance broker who was a city councillor and prominent member of the Citizens' League.

At its first meeting the committee agreed to send three members and the secretary to London to visit the Woolwich Arsenal to see what work had to be done, and to find out what the ministry expected of them. In the interim the committee agreed to carry out a survey of the city to find out what facilities and machinery was already available that could be used for making munitions. During their visit to London the committee was asked to consider extending its remit to cover the whole of Cumberland. A meeting with industrialists from the west of the county on 30 June unearthed strong opposition to that suggestion. This delayed the process until a further meeting with the ministry led to an agreement that west Cumberland should have its own committee and that of Carlisle should encompass the city and east Cumberland.

A meeting in July appointed Theodore Carr, James Morton, Richard Denman MP and Mr Pearson of Cowans Sheldon as an executive to pursue the site and buildings for a factory. A plan to take over one of the engineering works failed but the War Office agreed to the use of the Rifle Drill Hall, rent free, for the duration of the war. An agreement was signed on 18 September and a subsequent agreement to use the Artillery Hall for storage enabled the establishment of munitions manufacture in the city.

The city council provided electric generators and in late November the first twelve women were trained for a week in making shells. Further groups were trained in the following weeks and by the end of December production began, with the women who had been trained assisted by volunteers who had engineering experience, although many were rusty not having worked machines for twenty or thirty years. Men over the age for military service volunteered as labourers and a number of the local clergy were taken on as quality checkers. Some men of the cloth later became labourers and one vicar was a shell stamper from the date of the opening of the factory until it closed.

Under the Defence of the Realm Act (DORA) the sale of drink could be restricted or banned in areas near docks, barracks and

East Cumberland Shell Factory in the Drill Hall. Denis Perriam

Main machine shop in the Drill Hall. Denis Perriam

munitions factories. Concern was expressed that as Carlisle had joined the list of cities making munitions it would immediately come under the restrictions. Richard Denman MP calmed the panic:

> *'If Carlisle should become a 'munitions area' within the official meaning of the term the further regulation of the sale of drink will depend on the self-respect and good sense of the men themselves. It will be greatly to the credit of the city if restrictions are found to be unnecessary.'*

Memories of the Quintinshill train crash were stirred when, in the middle of June, a further twenty-one men travelled from hospitals in Carlisle to Edinburgh. Space having been created in the Infirmary, two men moved there from the County Hotel to join thirty-nine other survivors; in total fifty-nine casualties were still in the city.

Although life was becoming more hectic the papers naturally continued to headline and give details of action abroad, notably in the

Dardanelles. Lists of the men killed, wounded and missing were published. In the period between 1 May and 1 July 332 men of the Border Regiment were killed; 1 Border lost 148 men in the Dardanelles, of whom three had been born in Carlisle and two were resident in the city. Of the 148 men lost from 2 Border in France nine had been born and enlisted in Carlisle. Carlisle lost a further twelve men who were serving in other regiments and had been born in or lived locally. One of these was Lieutenant Basil Dixon of the 5th Battalion, Loyal North Lancashire Regiment. Aged twenty-five, he was the son of the Mayor of Carlisle and had attended Carlisle Grammar School.

Carlisle had a reputation as a noisy city. The sirens and hooters from factories calling men and women to start their shifts added to the less regular, but very frequent sounds of the railway engines steaming and whistling, carriages and trucks being shunted. These noises were added to by the regular bugles and trumpets used to rally and give commands to the troops in the Castle and those billeted in the city. The Reveille was sounded each morning at 5.30am by a trumpeter of the Yeomanry. He began at Chapel Street, moved into Lowther Street, then to the station, the Town Hall and finished at Scotch Street. Each call lasted three minutes so anyone living within those areas would find it impossible to avoid. Calls later in the day summoned the guard to parade outside the Town Hall. In the evening the guard was called at 6.50pm and the Lights Out sounded from the same five places as Reveille was called from 10.15pm.

The Munitions Act imposed regulations on the city. Trade union restrictions on working hours and practices would be suspended in the munitions works and any disputes referred to a court of arbitration. Employers would be prevented from poaching men from other companies. If workers constantly lost time or were absent they would be dealt with by munitions courts. The supply of labour was critical and not only would the local committees be ensuring that skilled men were able to do their work and provide sufficient unskilled labour to support them, the army would be releasing engineers and mechanics from the battalions they had joined earlier in the war as their contribution to armaments was more valuable. The unions had agreed to support the Bill, and the limitation on their powers, if the profits from munitions went to the government and not to the owners of the businesses involved.

This move not only enabled the local committee in Carlisle to continue its work with even more vigour, it encouraged men and women to volunteer, through the Citizens' League, to work in the industry. The League was pursuing its plan for a Roll of Honour which would list every man who had already signed up, and those who were eligible but had not yet volunteered. It now added a section to the form which would allow people to list service in the munitions factories as another option.

The debate about conscription to the military and vital industries still raged on, opponents arguing that if it was introduced the government would not only be able to recruit the numbers of men needed, but could also regulate the price paid. Unions were of the view that while men were prepared to volunteer, and firms to support them by keeping jobs open and making up wages, there was no benefit to the working man to support conscription. If everyone had to go employers would be less likely to support them and families would have to survive on a soldier's wage or widow's pension.

Towards the end of June the Lonsdale Battalion moved from the hutted accommodation of Prees Heath to a tented camp in Wensleydale. Headlined in the paper as 'A FORETASTE OF A SOLDIERS ROUGH LIFE' the article described the move, from being played out of the camp near Whitchurch in Shropshire by the pipes of the Highland Light Infantry and after a six-hour rail journey being greeted at Wensleydale by the pipes of another Highland battalion. Eventually the formerly quiet dale became home to 12,000 men housed in tents which filled the fields in the valley. Judging by the report in the paper life in camp was not particularly arduous. It told of men bathing in the river, playing cricket in the evening, using equipment sent over by Carlisle cricket club and hindering the battalion mascot, a greyhound, in its pursuit of local hares.

On 23 June the inquest was re-opened at Carlisle Town Hall on twenty-seven of those killed at Quintinshill. Meakin, the night duty signalman at Gretna gave his evidence about Tinsley travelling on the passenger train, and about the telegraph messages he had received signalling the movement of the trains involved. The reported presence of three others in the box, the firemen from the local goods and local passenger trains and the brakesman from the Welsh empties who were discussing the progress of the war with Meakin, caused further distraction.

Coroner's jury at Quintinshill. Ashley Kendall

Tinsley freely admitted he 'forgot about the passenger train' although he had just got off it. Although this sequence of events was accepted for many years it has been challenged in the recently published *Quintinshill Conspiracy* in which the authors point to confusion in the standing instructions to the signalmen and to other evidence not presented at the time.

In his summing up to the jury the coroner reminded them that while they were dealing with twenty-seven deaths, which was certainly the highest number ever dealt with in one case in the city by any coroner's jury, they needed to remember that in fact six or seven times that number had been killed and many more injured in the crash. He outlined the system used to ensure safety on the railway and the duty of railwaymen to carry out their duties safely.

The jury quickly decided that the deaths were the result of gross negligence on the part of both signalmen and the fireman of the passenger train. Mr Lightfoot, a Carlisle solicitor who was appearing for the railwaymen, warned the coroner against taking the next obvious step which was to commit the three men for trial on charges of manslaughter, since the offence, if any, had taken place in Scotland and Meakin had already been arrested and was to stand trial in that country.

Food supplies remained critical and the government resisted calls to regulate the price of some key items, notably flour, sugar and coal.

The minister responsible, Walter Runciman, said that the government had bought quantities of sugar to ensure supplies. They wanted to leave market forces to regulate the price of other items but looked to millers and coal owners to play their part and not make excessive profits, otherwise the government would intervene.

The recruiting office for munitions workers opened, but the number arriving to register was small. Most engineers were already involved in the production of some form of war materials. Officials were unable to decide whether the current work was of equal importance to the production of shells. Employers were reluctant to release skilled employees.

The war also caused the cancellation of Carlisle races, and in consequence the traditional week's holiday was put off for the employees of many companies. Some factories did close, but those engaged in war production remained in operation. The Boys' Brigade held their annual camp at Allonby but the activities were fewer than in previous years. Sports day was held with visitors arriving and although the boys had offered to help the local farmers to get in the hay crop, the weather had prevented this being completed.

Hospital trains were becoming more frequent at the station and the local Voluntary Aid Detachments and Boy Scouts kept them supplied

Drivers and firemen involved in the Quintinshill crash at the inquest. Left to right: John Graham, Andrew Johnson, fireman and driver of the second engine of the northbound express. Thomas Ingram, brakesman of the goods train from Carlisle, David Wallace, driver of the local passenger train, William Young, brakesman of the Welsh coal train, George Hutchinson, fireman on the local passenger train and David Todhunter, fireman of the lead engine on the northbound express. Cumbrian Newspapers Ltd

with refreshments provided by local people. On 28 June one hospital train bound for Glasgow passed through at 7pm and at 8.30pm another train pulled into the station, this one carrying 120 men bound for local hospitals. All the men could sit up and walk and were transferred from the train to the hospitals and homes within half an hour. Local doctors assisted with the transfer and taxi companies and individuals like Mr Chance, Sir Benjamin Scott, Dr Edwards and Mr Hutchinson, among others, lent their cars in which the patients were escorted to hospital accompanied by a member of the VAD.

The names and regiments of men were listed in the paper and most of them came from some distance, many from London and the south of England. This reflects the way the military authorities paid little attention to enabling families to visit the men. When a hospital ship arrived in Southampton the men were simply loaded onto the next available train regardless of its destination. A soldier of 10th Battalion, Royal Fusiliers returning wounded from France described in a letter home how on arrival in Southampton he had 'missed by a fluke a train to Carlisle or some impossible place'. His family lived in Coventry and when he ended up in a hospital in the east end of London he might have preferred Carlisle.

Anger at 'German Aliens' led to action by the authorities. Five Germans were arrested in Carlisle and sent to internment camp. Four of the men were butchers and one a confectioner who had been in the workhouse.

To pay for the war the government in December 1914 instituted a scheme of war loans which enabled people to loan money which would be repaid, with interest, at the end of hostilities. Local firms like Laings offered its employees the opportunity to pay £4 to buy a loan bond worth £5. Morton's offered a similar arrangement, but it would cost the employee £4 15s. Other companies offered similar deals and put money into the scheme themselves. In October the Cumberland Motor Cycle Club voted to allocate some of its funds to an investment in war loan.

Local appeals for support for organisations involved in the war were in every edition of the paper. Clothing for soldiers and prisoners of war, sandbags, eggs for soldiers in the local hospitals and 'treats' were collected and distributed by the Citizens' League. The Red Cross, in September, reported that a total of £290 (about £19,000 in 2013) had been spent on refreshments for the 10,510 soldiers who had passed through the station on hospital trains. In addition 476 soldiers had been treated in the local auxiliary hospitals and 183 casualties from the Quintinshill train crash had been cared for. Support for soldiers' families and for the men returning injured was taking more time and 'men of leisure' were asked to call at the League's offices to offer their services.

The national registration scheme, which would require every man to record his occupation and availability, was debated in parliament. The fear at the outbreak of war was that too few men would enlist so anyone who volunteered was accepted. The Act was passed on 15 July and required all men of military age not already serving in the forces, to register and list their occupation. The result of this census, published in September showed that there were almost five million men of military age not in the services of whom 1.6 million were in what were termed 'starred' occupations who would not be called up as their employment was more important.

In his annual report to the Health Committee Dr Beard gave the statistics for births and deaths in the city in 1914. The death rate, at 16.1 per 1,000 was above the national average and was also higher that the average rate of the 145 smaller towns with which Carlisle was compared. A comment in his report caused anger among some farmers. He said that while the milk and meat produced in Carlisle was 'clean', that is free from tuberculosis (TB) some from outside was diseased. The argument ran on for some months, with the farmers presenting evidence that the doctor was mistaken. A counter-argument was presented by a local butcher:

> *'If your readers would visit our local market on a Monday they would hear the auctioneer call out when certain cattle are to be sold "not insured" or "sold to go away only" which means in plain words that "no Carlisle butcher should buy this beast as it is thought to be diseased". I think the meeting had forgotten that it was only quite recently that a number of local farmers were heavily fined for disposing of diseased cattle.'*

The sanitary inspector's report included a census of some of the services found in Carlisle in 1915. Along with forty-five bakehouses, forty-four cow keepers and milk sellers, twenty-eight fish and fried potato shops and seven ice cream parlours there were three common lodging houses.

The attack on 'shirkers' from the city and country was the topic of a meeting held outside the recruiting office in Devonshire Street on the eve of the first anniversary of the outbreak of the war. Married men had volunteered in good numbers, it was the ones aged between eighteen and twenty-five who were missing. The speaker, Sergeant Major Jones, said what he was complaining about:

> *'These men have resisted the most piteous and plaintive appeals. Perhaps when the register* [National Registration] *is completed the young beggars will be located. The complaint is against two classes of young men, the shop assistants and the farmers' sons. In Cumberland the miners, and scavengers and workers in many industries have turned up well but there is a large number of young fellows who are afraid to get their skins wet or scratched.'*

One of the activities restricted by the Defence of the Realm Act was the keeping of pigeons. The potential for these to be used to pass messages to an enemy had not been overlooked and pigeon fanciers had to register their birds. The Chief Constable prosecuted an owner, the second to appear in court in a fortnight, for failing to have a permit. Mrs Kidd of Granville Road was looking after pigeons for her son who lived in Edinburgh. She had applied late for a permit to keep eight birds but when a constable visited the loft he found fifteen birds there. The defence was that seven of them had been up for sale and were no longer at the loft but the magistrate, the Mayor, said that if people were not going to abide fully by the act they could expect to be punished. He was allowed to impose a fine of up to £100. The last offender had been fined 10s 6d and Mrs Kidd was going to be fined twice that, one guinea (£1 1s) with costs and if there was another case the fine would again be doubled.

During July more land was requisitioned to the north of Carlisle for HM Factory, Gretna, the UK's largest cordite factory in the First World War. The volume of construction work put huge pressure on the local building firms who lost men to the works just ten miles away and the overall impact on the city was huge. Once the factory opened it soon employed more than 15,000 workers, rising to over 19,000 by 1917.

The majority of these, sixty per cent, were young women from all parts of northern England and Scotland. The labourers building the factory visited Carlisle for 'recreation' and many took up lodgings. Once the factory was in production the girls were lodged in hotels and other places in the city, they were transported to work on the railway and in their leisure hours they sought entertainment. From this time on the effect of the factory put huge pressure on the services, and good will of the city.

Many of those who arrived early in the creation of Gretna were labourers but as the factory opened some conscripts arrived from other parts of the country, many medically unfit for active service. One such was Harry Mills, aged 20, who had very poor eyesight. He was classified as B3, fit only for sedentary work which could have taken him abroad but he was dispatched to Gretna from his home in Stoke where he had been employed as a grocer's errand boy and then in the local pottery industry. Some men lived in hostels but many more took lodgings, as Harry did when he moved into 41 Adelaide Street where his landlady was Mrs Anderson. Postcards sent to Harry have been kept by his family; the first to him in Carlisle is dated 27 August 1915.

Painters employed at Gretna. Ashley Kendall

The date of arrival of the first women at Gretna is less certain but one woman, Jean [always called Jeanie by her family] Anderson was typical of many. Aged twenty-two when war was declared Jeanie had always lived in the Carlisle area. Her father had been a forester and had also worked on the railway as a fireman. With a sister Annie, Jeanie moved with her family to Dalston and by 1911 was employed as a general domestic servant at Randalinton Farm, Longtown. Whether she was still there as war broke out and later as Gretna first developed, is unknown but she would certainly have known the site as Randalinton is on the southern boundary of the Gretna/Longtown complex.

Card sent to Harry Mills when he was in Carlisle, his medical category was B3. John Hughes

Although difficult to find a precise figure it is probable that Jeanie earned at most about 10s (50p) a week as a domestic servant. Once the Gretna factory began women were employed for an initial wage of 15s (75p) rising to about £2 10s (£2.50p) once they had completed four weeks training. This was more than many men and certainly more than women in the factories of Carlisle were able to earn. Jeanie's postcards were also kept by her family, one sent on 10 August 1915 records her address in Carlisle as 3 Tilbury Road. Jeanie and Harry feature later in the story.

Another change in legislation was brought about by the Munitions in War Act in July 1915 which required workers to obtain leaving certificates to change jobs. Although not hugely important in Carlisle at first, there were a few instances of carpenters and bricklayers falling foul of the legislation as they tried to leave local firms. It became very important once Gretna got into production and many workers tried to double or even quadruple their wages by moving from building, engineering, domestic service or small firm employment to the government-funded wages paid for munitions workers. The position of farmers was made even more difficult as they had to compete with the wages offered to both male and female workers as well as the demands of the military and conscription for their sons and male workers to go to the war.

Opportunities for entertainment increased when on 29 July the New Picture House opened in Botchergate. With mock classical pillars, ornate flooring, a tea room, a waiting lounge, five-piece orchestra and state of the art ventilation, it provided an exotic but respectable setting for the new form of entertainment. Illustrations showed it with uniformed staff and patrons elegantly dressed. Just down the road, still in Botchergate, the Stanley Hall offered comfortable seats on a wooden balcony but those sitting in the stalls made do with wooden chairs. The Star in Denton Holme was more basic, described in the *Journal* as somewhere shop and factory girls could go without having to dress up for the occasion.

Women were increasingly taking on jobs traditionally done by men. The *Journal* wrote about lady postmen delivering letters and parcels in some parts of the city and surrounding area.

Sir Robert and Lady Baden-Powell inspected Scouts and Guides in Carlisle in early September. Fifty scouts and eight scoutmasters had joined the army. Those remaining had been fully involved with war activities in the city. Some had studied first aid and ambulance work, signalling and pioneering. Baden-Powell congratulated the scouts on their work in bridge guarding, acting as messengers and helping at the station. He was particularly impressed that some had offered to help at Quintinshill without waiting for orders. On leaving the scouts at the park the Baden-Powells went to Charlotte Street Congregational Church to speak to the four companies of Girl Guides, about eighty in number. Sir Robert mentioned an incident when the Lonsdale Battalion was leaving Carlisle and a lady in the crowd fell and broke her shoulder blade. A guide offered first aid and was complimented by the doctor who dealt with the case who said that it had been bound up as well as he could have done.

It was hoped that an abortive attack on 16 August on a chemical works near Lowca in west Cumberland by a German U-boat would encourage more volunteers. However, recruitment slowed during September with, in one week, only twenty-six men offering themselves for service, and twenty-three in the week following. That these weeks were soon after the forms for the national register had been collected did not indicate an increased sense of duty among the young men. There was an opportunity for men between the ages of forty and fifty to join the Territorial Association battalion for home service only. Recruiting was opened in Carlisle and other towns in the two counties. Four hundred younger men aged between nineteen and forty were also needed to boost the ranks of 3/4 Border which was in training. It was hoped that this would attract men from Carlisle as a number of men from the city were already in the battalion.

An empty hospital train attracted large crowds to the Citadel station. The new train, built by the Caledonian Railway was on a tour of Scotland and the north of England; each of the 7,850 visitors paid a minimum of 1s to enter. The train was a great improvement with space for 144 cot patients and 202 sitting up, and an area for infectious patients who could be kept in isolation. It also had a pharmacy, kitchen, a rest car for the doctors and nurses travelling with the patients and store rooms.

The government's budget in late September resulted in price increases in tea, sugar and tobacco. Tea went up by 4d a pound, sugar prices increased by a halfpenny per pound. Retailers in the city thought that the price of cigarette tobacco would increase by at least 2s, but they feared the manufacturers might add a little more to cover their costs.

At the end of September the munitions tribunal, intended to control the flow of labour from essential work, held its first meeting in the city. Men, and later women, wanting to take up a job in a new company had first to be granted a leaving certificate. Mr Thomas Strong, coroner at the Quintinshill inquest was in the chair, with Mr John Dove for the employers and Mr Creegen for the unions. The first cases typified the issues facing the employers and men. Thomas Irving, a labourer working for the railway engineers Tyers wanted to leave to work at Gretna. Irving had a certificate from his doctor saying that he would benefit from working in a country environment. His employer said that he had taken Irving on when he was pleading for work, at first he was paid 15s a week, which was increased to 23s with a 4s war bonus, and he then moved onto piece work where he earned 34s. He was working in their packing department on war materials, most of his time was in the open and he had not been off through sickness. Tyers had lost about one third of their men to the army and four more of their engineers to Gretna. The Chairman refused to issue a leaving certificate.

Workmen from Gretna became increasingly obvious in the city. There were court reports of drunkenness on Saturday night. Fines were imposed at a higher level than for men not employed at Gretna. Conditions of work there were the subject of a workmen's meeting held on 2 October at the Queen's Hall. There were complaints that the rates of pay promised when they were recruited did not materialise when they began work. Men had come from some distances to work and married men had to send money to their wives and families as well as paying for their own lodgings. The train service from Gretna to Carlisle was inadequate; workers had to wait for between one and a half and up to three hours at a station with no facilities. Some workers had been offered payment for travelling time but this was stopped after two days. The length and structure of the working day also caused disagreement, the men wanted to work for nine hours a day during the week and five hours on a Saturday.

To replace those killed and wounded in the fighting it was estimated that the army needed in the region of 30,000 men each week, many more than the number of willing volunteers. Later in October Lord Derby, the Director of Recruiting, announced that his scheme was to ask those not engaged on war work, to account for why they were not volunteering for the army. He hoped that by regular canvassing sufficient men would be persuaded to sign up. Not everyone was convinced that there were many 'shirkers' and those opposing conscription challenged Lord Derby to publish the number of those eligible for service.

Losses in France and Gallipoli continued with two or three columns of the *Journal* filled with names of those killed and wounded. *Soldiers Died in the Great War* identifies twenty-eight men born in Carlisle killed between 1 September and 31 October. A prominent family faced with loss was that of the High Sheriff of Cumberland and cotton manufacturer, Frederick Chance and his wife Mary, whose 32-year-old son, Captain Andrew Chance, was killed by a shell in France.

The costs of essential foodstuffs rose during September by an average of three and a half per cent, with tea and sugar each going up by around fourteen per cent. Butter was up seven per cent, milk five per cent and fish four per cent. When compared with prices at the outbreak of the war the price of meat was up by forty per cent as was the price of flour and bread which had increased by just under that figure. The grocers thought that while the large suppliers might be able to sell at the government prices those selling smaller amounts would have to be supported as they could not sell sugar at a loss. The Carlisle grocers resented that the prices quoted for many commodities were those charged in London. They argued that as most of the imported food arrived in London docks dealers and shopkeepers there did not have to pay extra to transport it as they did.

The Liquor Control Regulations published on 14 October were not a real surprise to anyone when it covered large parts of the region. There had been increasing concern, not just among the temperance movement, at the increase in drink-related violence and disruptive behaviour, particularly among the workers from Gretna. Attempts by licensees to limit the size of the controlled districts had eventually been defeated as chief constables and magistrates did not want the boundaries of the control area to permit for easy travel to non-controlled areas for fear of the problems seen in Carlisle and around Gretna spreading to their districts.

As ever the Citizens' League was quick to address the problem and set up a committee to look at ways in which Gretna men could be provided with suitable entertainment to divert them from the pubs. They also decided to try to resurrect the idea of a restroom for soldiers and sailors travelling at night. Many were seen sleeping on the platform and some sort of refuge with food and drink would be appreciated. Ladies from the League had offered to run the restroom if the station authorities would give them space.

Hare coursing was a popular sport and the Border Coursing Union complained that the building of the huge factory would prevent any hare coursing on the previously very successful land between the rivers Gretna and Esk, particularly the mosslands. Whether the meetings could be continued at all was uncertain but at the meeting on 20 and 21 October, although the organisers feared a poor attendance because men had joined the army, the level of support to see the greyhounds chasing the hares was as big, perhaps bigger, than in previous years.

The munitions regulations caught out a Carlisle night school teacher of engineering who volunteered in all his holidays for work at Leyland, the vehicle builders in Lancashire. The company knew he was a teacher who was helping with war work in his summer holiday. With the increase in munitions work in the city he thought he would be able to transfer home to do war work during the day without harming his evening job. Leyland took him to the Blackburn munitions tribunal where he was told that he should remain at Leyland and the tribunal would write to Carlisle to ask that his job be kept open for him.

Another confusion arose over the Derby starring scheme. While skilled farm labourers had been marked as indispensable a to agriculture no farmer had been starred. Letters had been received by a number of farmers asking them to enlist. Lord Derby, in a speech in the middle of November, said that where a farmer occupied and farmed his own land he would be marked as indispensable and would not be called up. In the same speech on 19 November he said that although the deadline for the scheme had been 30 November it had been extended to 11 December.

The competition for workers was exemplified by the fact that the wages at the half-yearly Martinmas Hirings were the highest ever, confirming the need for skilled labour to work the land. The added benefit to some, it was suggested, would have been the possibility that as farm workers they would be starred as essential employees. The ending of contracts meant that some farm labourers took the opportunity to volunteer and over a four-day period some 300 men were attested and more were still arriving at the recruiting offices.

Carlisle was the centre for final selection for the whole county and it was noted that the rate of rejections were rising. One town, which was not named in the paper, had been sending men in great numbers but of the current volunteers nearly two out of five were being sent home with a certificate to record that they had volunteered, but been rejected. Voluntary recruitment continued to rise and in the middle of October 564 men applied in one week, the best figure since the start of the war.

November 13 was designated 'Our Day' and an opportunity for the Red Cross to hold collections to support work with wounded men in France, at base hospitals, and at home. Three hundred women collected money all over the city, selling a variety of flags and badges and illuminated cards to be displayed in house windows. It wasn't just the sale of flags that raised money. Hetheringtons the auctioneers offered to sell any item for the fund without charging their fee. A pet fox and

Flags sold on 'Our Day' by members of the Citizens' League raising £400 (£26,000 today). Denis Perriam

a goat were resold many times, raising between them £24, a 22lb cheese sold for £2 17s and ducks, hens, geese and potatoes were also sold. The three flag days in the city since the start of the war had collected a total of £1,161 (£77,000 in 2013), with each one achieving a higher total than the one before, so the will to give, in spite of rising prices, was still there.

Two days earlier on the 11th Lord Lonsdale had travelled to Codford to bid farewell to the Lonsdale battalion which had been ordered to France. He told the men how proud he was of them and of his association with them. He spoke of Colonel Machell and how he had confidence that he would lead the battalion well. A march past and celebratory lunch concluded the events of the morning and Lord Lonsdale left the men to return north.

The drink restrictions came into force on Monday, 22 November. The hours of opening of public houses were limited to between noon and 2.30pm and 6pm and 9pm on weekdays, all public houses in the city were closed on Sunday. Non-intoxicating drinks and food could be served all day, part of the attempt to make the public house more of a family environment rather than the male dominated drinking den that it had been. No 'treating' was allowed and water could be added to whisky in a proportion which would have led to severe penalties under previous legislation.

Zeppelin raids had been damaging east and south coast towns and London since the spring. The Carlisle press frequently carried reports on the raids and the damage and loss of life caused. Nationally restrictions on lighting had been imposed and the illumination from street lights in Carlisle was reduced by only having one light in two turned on, but those at street corners were retained for safety reasons.

Women continued to take an increasingly central role in industrial and commercial life. A lengthy leader in the *Journal* on 19 November went into detail quoting reports from national papers on the way in which women were viewed in the workplace:

> *'Who could have dreamed before the war that factories turning out high explosive shells would be manned solely by women without the slightest experience of fast running machinery? Men in the trade laughed at the idea. Wherever women have been employed output is constantly increasing and there is no sign of it abating.'*

Fashion remained important and there were adverts for both men's and women's clothing throughout the war.

Although towns like Kendal, Penrith and Workington continued to provide many recruits, the number from Carlisle had increased to ensure the city was at this stage providing the greatest proportion. Men were still arriving to join 4 Border, but on being told that there were no vacancies left the office without signing. The canvass for the registration scheme was still progressing slowly in the city

Fashion advert in Carlisle Journal 1915. Cumbrian Newspapers Ltd

as not enough people had offered to distribute and collect the cards. There was still doubt that the voluntary scheme would work and in a speech at the Stock Exchange even Lord Derby echoed the concerns when he warned that many more would have to come forward if the scheme was to be proved effective and conscription avoided. An important part of the voluntary scheme was the creation of military tribunals, not to be confused with the munititions tribunal which would make decisions when a man wished to be placed in a later group than the one he was in, or for employers to appeal to retain essential workers. The rate of failure at medical remained relatively high and a number of men, it was said, attended to be rejected because of their essential jobs, but they would now get an armband to show that they were on war service.

Most of the Belgians who had arrived in November 1914 had now found work and were living in rooms in the city At the end of November the secretary of the Belgians' Refugee Committee announced that Rickerby House was closing and that the furniture people had loaned twelve months before had, where this was possible,

Crowd outside the Town Hall to see the German Gun captured by 2 Border during the Battle of Loos. Ashley Kendall

been returned. However, there were some items which had lost the identification marks and if anyone wanted to call at the house on 30 November they could claim it.

The annual Christmas celebrations arranged for the poor were, it was announced in the press in the first week of December, to be cancelled. Those who would normally benefit were no longer viewed as being destitute. Many families who used to attend were now receiving money from fathers or other family members in the army. Many families were renting out rooms, sometimes in multiple occupancy, to workmen from Gretna. When the war began the city authorities were concerned that there would be much destitution and the need to provide support to families, but this had not been the case.

One of the most successful war related charity events in December 1915 was that of the farmers to support the Red Cross. Farmers, their families and people from the city gathered in Harrison's Auction Mart. The fund was a national one for all farmers to contribute to and its founder, a man from Croydon, hoped to raise £250,000. In addition to the sheep, cattle and other livestock, some of which was sold more than once, purchasers went away with a motor car which had been entered by the vicar of Orton, a badger, shirts, blouses, cheeses and two kittens. Competitions such as guess the name of the kitten, weight of a pig or the amount raised in the sale attracted many. The sale raised just over £4,000 which at that stage in the collection was the largest amount for any single event.

Crowds went into the city on 2 December to see the German field gun captured by men of 2 Border at Hulluch during the Battle of Loos on 25 September. The parade was an opportunity to demonstrate support for the war and involved not only the Border Regiment, but also the Volunteer Corps, companies of the Boys Brigade and troops of Boy Scouts. A local cameraman filmed the parade as it moved between solid crowds of cheering people from the Castle Gate, along Corporation Road, the Sands, Lowther Street, the Crescent, and English Street to the Market Square. The route was lined by men from 3/4 Border and the police including some special constables. The Town Hall steps were crowded, as were the surrounding streets and people watched from the upstairs windows of the buildings around the square.

The Citizens' League was also busy organising comforts for the

The German gun in Carlisle Castle in 1915. Denis Perriam

troops. Men in France and the Dardanelles and prisoners of war in Germany were hoping for warm clothing, sweets, cigarettes and tobacco, condensed milk, tinned cocoa and coffee, tea, pipes, coloured handkerchiefs, soap and shaving soap. The Citizens' League posted 117 parcels to men at the front and so far as they were aware every man from the city who was a PoW would be receiving a parcel in time for Christmas. Three families had received financial support from the Soldiers' Help Society. A longer term benefit for troops travelling through Carlisle was opened on 8 December. The Citizens' League had co-ordinated efforts to provide rest and refreshment for soldiers and sailors who had to change trains at Citadel Station. The new rest room in Court Square was fitted out by local tradesmen who gave their labour free; other people provided furniture, soft furnishing and kitchen utensils. Both facilities were to be run by 100 women who had volunteered to the League and 100 men from the Voluntary Training Corps who would all work in shifts to keep both facilities open for twenty-four hours every day.

Men in the local hospitals were provided with regular entertainment by amateur performers, many of them children, who sang, recited and danced. Choirs toured the hospitals singing seasonal songs and carols.

The tram company had agreed to put collection boxes on each of their vehicles and the Boys' Brigade toured the city collecting magazines and books. The weekly egg collection for men in hospital had not done well in the weeks before Christmas, as this was not a time when chickens could be relied upon to lay.

The final week of the Derby Scheme enrolment saw huge crowds collecting each day outside the offices in Devonshire Street. Complaints from the men about having to queue were countered with the comment that they should not have left it until the 11th hour to attest. A second office was opened in Lonsdale Street and additional officers were brought in to help. One reason put forward for the last minute rush was the realisation by starred men that they had to be on the list to ensure their case came before the tribunal. Officers went to Gretna to deal with the many cases of men there who would otherwise

Rest Room provided by George and Joblin Car Dealers of Carlisle who had planned to use it as a showroom. Open 24 hours a day it was staffed by members of the Citizens' League. Denis Perriam

have swelled the crowds in Carlisle. In the following week arm bands were issued to all men who had attested. These were to be worn at all times, though not everyone complied with this requirement, and showed the group to which the man belonged and his registration number. The official announcement by the Prime Minister of the number of men recruited across the whole country was scheduled for 14 December, but was postponed because owing to the rush in the last week the final number could not be calculated in time. There was a spirit of optimism among those in Carlisle who opposed conscription.

At the Citizens' League meeting in the week before Christmas it was reported that the refreshment room at the station and the rest room in Court Square were much busier than had been anticipated. In the first ten days between 4,000 and 5,000 men had made use of one or both of the facilities. Day and night men were to be seen taking refreshment, resting or sleeping as they waited for their connections. Trying to maintain a supply of pies, the most popular item on the menu, had been challenging and one day through a misunderstanding at a local hotel 250 men of the Border Regiment had to be served lunch. The League's concert on 20 December was well attended and raised about £83 for the Soldiers and Sailors Help Fund.

The Derby scheme went into its next phase with the dates for the call-up of the first groups of men being set from 20 January. The arrangements were spelled out in the papers to assist those administering the scheme, and to explain to men who wanted to appear before tribunals how to go about it.

For most who lived in Carlisle Christmas was a much quieter festival than before the war. The limitations on the availability of alcohol, the absence of many men, and the employment of women all meant that the season was very different. People spent their holiday in visiting relatives, or helping in the hospitals, canteens or with the Vynne-Latimer dinner or Reeves tea, both events for older residents rather than the poor. The papers contained long lists of those who had donated gifts and presents of food to the patients in the hospitals around the city. Convalescent soldiers were taken out or invited to people's homes for Christmas meals. Groups visited each of the hospitals to sing carols and distribute small presents. The workhouse was virtually empty as the poor who were physically capable of work could all easily find some form of employment. Special trains had been laid on for the workmen from Gretna to allow them to get home for the Christmas and New Year holidays.

There was a bad side however as on Christmas Day the amount of drunkenness was, in the words of the Chief Constable, 'shocking'. He acknowledged that the public houses were closed, but was concerned that many of those arrested had been collecting and storing drink in the preceding weeks before restrictions were fully imposed.

There was a claim that the employment of women in jobs previously done by men was resulting in wages being depressed, but this was denied by management. The arguments centred on the employment of young women in preparation for dealing with the loss of men to the Derby scheme, and the fact that women were judged, by union or management, as being unable to do the same work as men so, asked the employers, why should the union be demanding equal pay? The whole issue of the effect of the increasing number of women already in employment, and the certainty that the numbers would increase was of concern particularly to the unions. Some said that as the women had been taken on to replace men at war they should have their employment automatically terminated when the men returned. The union correspondent in the *Journal* took the view that women would continue in employment after the war and therefore the issue was not about them taking the place of men but rather the need to organise them so that they were not used as an excuse to reduce wages for all.

The press was involved in keeping the populace informed of what would now be termed as frequently asked questions about conscription and tribunals. The men who did not receive call-up letters were told that they could assume they were registered as starred. Others had to apply to the tribunals before 30 December if they wanted to claim that their services were essential to employers, but were warned that the decision was not theirs, or their employers, but would be made by the tribunal on behalf of the state. The tribunal would hear statements from the man, his employer and either his union representative, or somebody able to represent the 'working man'.

There was continued opposition to the war by some in Carlisle as demonstrated by a meeting on 28 December. Mr James Scott Duckers, who had been brought up in Wetheral but was living and working in London as a solicitor, was the chairman of the Stop-the-War campaign and a conscientious objector. He addressed a meeting of the Independent Labour Party in the city. His story became a *cause celèbre*, mainly because he wrote a book about his experiences. As his case was dealt with in London it is not directly part of the story of Carlisle, but because of his association with the area he was influential to men in the city with similar views.

The City Council accepted the gift of a motor ambulance, presented by Canon Rawnsley who had raised the money from local individuals and firms to buy the chassis with the body donated by James Hodgson, a motor builder with a garage on West Walls.

The end of 1915 saw most people in Carlisle with a more positive view of the future than they had held at the end of 1914, although concern for the increasing number from the city at the front remained huge. The citizens were prepared to support the war effort, contributing to flag days, giving their time to entertain troops and convalescent servicemen. Ladies rallied round to help with the preparation and running of hospitals and homes. Women took up employment and the phenomenon of the working mother appeared as never before. Gifts were given to troops passing through the station and those staying in the city. The new rest room was fully staffed and provided an invaluable service to soldiers and sailors passing through the station. Most significantly the population of the district had increased by 20,000 putting huge pressures on housing and other services. Many of the newcomers were single men working on the building of the munition works at Gretna. They needed lodgings, transport to work and entertainment.

There had been times of tragedy and sadness. The Quintinshill train crash had cost many lives including some from Carlisle, but had shown the populace prepared to help in many different ways. Over 150 men who had been born or lived in the city had died in the war during the year, including the sons of the Mayor and the High Sheriff of the County. The Border Regiment had over 1,300 men killed and both the city and regiment had many more men who had been wounded, some so badly that their lives and those of their families would be changed for ever. Even in this tragedy, however, the Citizens' League and City Council were trying to help by urging employers to identify jobs that could be done by wounded and disabled men.

What might the New Year bring? Hospital trains continued to be met by members of the Red Cross and VAD. Boy scouts and other uniformed organisations gave support, the Volunteer Defence Force prepared for a possible conflict on home soil. New structures and institutions, like Gretna and the Central Control Board were embryonic in December 1915 but would take centre stage in the life of the city in 1916. Recruitment was going to change from the voluntary process of 1915 to a more controlled process through the Derby scheme. Tribunals for munitions and military service would become a regular feature of life, with conscientious objectors emerging.

The differences between urban and rural life would crystallise with continuing complaints from town dwellers that those in country districts were not playing their full part in joining the services, and those in the country concerned at the increased pressures for food production the implications of which were not understood by those in towns. Normality would be demonstrated by the work of the Watch Committee with regard to law and order and public safety and morals; the Education Committee and schools would continue to look after the needs of children and young people. Churches would care for their congregations and contribute to life in the city. Theatres and cinemas would provide entertainment, as would the public houses, albeit in a changed form. Sport would continue, the otter hounds, the hare coursing, bowling clubs and fishing would be supported by those left in the city. Other sports, notably football, would begin to broaden with the involvement of women teams from munitions and other factories taking part in charity matches.

CHAPTER 5

1916: Social Changes and Military Losses

Increase in drunkenness – Working conditions of munitions workers – Farmers and their sons – Pressure on housing – Air raid precautions – Alien registration – Military Tribunals – Trams – Conscientious Objectors – Shortages – Lighting Restrictions – Anti-German feeling – Introduction of summer time – Conscription – Hiring Fair – State control unfair – Whitsun cancelled – Public Health – Military success, more casualties – Lonsdales at the Somme – Opening of the Gretna Tavern – Gas and electricity supply – Women's football – Women police – Charity collections – Rest Room opens – Cases before the magistrates take on a new twist – Jobs for wounded soldiers – Public house control extended – Price increases and food shortages – Cinemas – Juvenile crime – More problems with the trams – Christmas puddings for the troops – A quiet Christmas – Death of a notable lady

January of 1916 was relatively quiet. One issue of the *Journal* had a column beginning with the phrase 'Little happened on the western front during the weekend', but this was just the lull of winter campaigning before the storm of the spring and summer offensives.

Soldiers' letters gave details of their experiences in the trenches. At home there was a decline in adult crime, but an increase in drunkenness and juvenile crime. The welfare of munitions workers and the pressure of seven day working was a cause of concern, as was the risk of illness caused by overcrowding. The Control Board took over public houses in Gretna, an indication of what may happen in Carlisle. The war was having an impact on the weaving and cloth printing companies, like Morton Sundour which before the war was dependent on German produced, and patented, aniline dyes.

The Compulsion Bill went through all stages in parliament becoming law before the end of the month. The Bill was not uncontested; the Trades Congress met in London and recommended that the Parliamentary Labour Party should oppose the Bill. Three government ministers resigned and Sir Richard Denman, Carlisle's MP who was undergoing officer training in London but still attended parliament, wrote with some pride in the local press that he was opposed to the Bill which, he said, had not been proved to be based on a secure basis of fact. Also he was against the forcing of young single men to serve before older married men. He was of the view that a man of twenty was of greater economic use to the country than a man of thirty or thirty-five.

Denman was not out to make himself popular in the city as he acknowledged that he was supporting a minority, something he had previously advised others not to do once a majority decision had been reached. In the final vote in parliament he was one of thirty-six MPs who sustained their objection to the Bill. He suffered a loss of popularity in the city, including his being removed from a vice presidency of Carlisle Golf Club.

The attestation process of the previous month resulted in 800,000 men coming forward, but a further 651,000 single men were, according to Lord Derby's committee, 'unaccounted for'. The recruiting offices opened again in mid-January to allow more men to register. There were assurances that it would not be used to force industrial conscription or allow employers to force men who were union activists into the army by saying to tribunals that they were non-essential workers. The first men to be called up were due to arrive at the Castle on Monday, 24 January and most answered the summons. The commencement of this process did not stop other men volunteering to enter specific regiments or trades and reasonable numbers continued to take this route.

Although there was a decline in serious crime, the growth in drunkenness was causing great concern across the city. In 1914 there had been 273 convictions for drunkenness; in 1915 the figure was 953. Early analysis of the figures suggested that the addresses of those

Card sent to Harry Mills, armbands showed the conscription group. John Hughes

Some in medical groups B and C were often designated as suitable only for sedentary work. John Hughes

convicted showed that the number from Carlisle had increased slightly but the vast majority came from outside of the city, notably Gretna. Each week there were twenty to thirty cases before the magistrates, and all but one or two were from or associated with the works there. The problems of drink were addressed by a circular which was issued under DORA making illegal the practice of treating soldiers to drinks. The recruiting officer for Carlisle, who was responsible for enforcing the regulation, also indicated that he would take action against those who gave bottles of whisky or other drink to men leaving home to join up or return to their regiments.

The rise in population led to demands increasing for entertainment and recreation. A report in the papers described the crowds in English

Street queuing to get into the New Picture House. The writer concluded that it was because of the pressure of work that all the picture houses did good business on a Saturday night. One picture house was full on Sunday too, with the congregation attracted by the Reverend George Bramwell Evans, the 31-year-old minister of the Carlisle Central Methodist Chapel. He decided to hold his services in the Botchergate Picture House and to provide good quality musical entertainment from known national performers.

Concern over the welfare of munitions workers led to a review of working practices. Most firms were under huge pressure to meet deadlines and volume. They had instituted seven day working with long shifts. After some months the amount of illness and absence had increased to a level that led to the review. It was suggested that men and women were working too many hours and were in need of time to relax and recuperate. Lloyd George sent a circular to all factories recommending that they discontinue work on Sundays and workers should have no more than twelve shifts in a fortnight. He wrote, 'It's better to work overtime in the week rather than Sunday shifts'.

The annual dinner of the Cumberland and Westmorland Agricultural Union attracted 190 members to the Crown and Mitre Hotel. At the beginning of his speech Canon Rawnsley expressed the opinion that every farmer was as much a combatant as a munitions worker or serviceman. However he then moved on to the criticism that farming areas had not sent sufficient men to the war. He had to agree that perhaps some areas were deficient but other dales had sent just about every able-bodied men they had. His sympathy was with the dales farmer who had worked himself up from labourer to tenant farmer, but was not able to pay for labourers so was dependent on family working with him.

He spoke about the way in which the Government was trying to ensure a supply of soldiers and went on:

> *'But the time is coming when these men* [dales farmers] *must make the sacrifice and when I reflect how many a strong farmer's lass might turn to if she would and fill the post of her brother so that he might go to the war. I ask these Cumberland lads and lasses to think what is happening in France at this moment. It is not too much to say that the whole of French agriculture is in the hands of women at the moment. .... "How*

> *splendid these women are", said my son as he watched the women ploughing and carting manure behind the English lines. Now I should like the French to say how splendid these English women are.*
>
> *'As I look round and see how all women in all ranks are serving their country as nurses, munitions workers, as war office clerks, as postwomen, tram conductors, managers of buffets, ticket collectors, motor drivers, hearse drivers, I feel the age of the super woman has arrived. All that we ask now is that women help us in agriculture.'*

The pressure on housing in the city became more intense as the number of labourers grew. Many labourers were in lodgings, some even sharing beds. Repeatedly the City Council tried to get funding to build more social housing but the Munitions Board would not agree that an increase was required. Many landladies did not allow the men staying in their houses to come in before a certain time in the evening and they were forced to find places to shelter, so they went to public houses.

Raids by Zeppelins were becoming more frequent along the east coast and particularly towards London and Kent. Occasional raids extended inland as far as the Midlands with casualties at Derby and Wolverhampton. Damage caused to buildings in Sunderland and up the Northumberland coast in 1915 made it clear that the German raiders were capable of navigating significant distances and it was feared that with the building of Gretna northern Cumberland, and therefore Carlisle, was likely to become a target. Some restrictions had been put in place in 1915 but the government and Carlisle City Council decided that more needed to be done. The lights of the city could, it was said, be clearly seen glowing from Port Carlisle over eleven miles away.

An emergency meeting of the Watch Committee established procedures to be followed to protect the city. The national regulation passed in February did not apply to Carlisle but the Town Clerk was instructed to request the Home Office to widen the area covered. Lights in shop windows and offices had to be kept dim with only a dull glow visible from outside. All external lights had to be turned off or at least shaded and covered if the Chief Constable considered they were necessary for public safety. A side effect of the lighting restriction was the cancelling by the council of licenses for late night dancing as it would be difficult for people to see their way home.

Another emergency procedure associated with the Gretna development was the extension of the Aliens Registration Order to cover north Cumberland and Carlisle. This required all foreign nationals from friendly, neutral or enemy states to obtain permission from the police to enter or remain in the area. It also required hotel and boarding house keepers to maintain a register of aliens staying in their premises; it was the responsibility of the hotelier to ensure that the person had registered with the police.

The processes for recruitment came into force in February and March, the call-up of single men was expected. The newly established military tribunals considered the cases of men applying to have their enlistment delayed as they were doing essential work. The tribunal members for Carlisle appointed by the City Council on 13 February had some familiar names amongst them: the Mayor (Mr Gibbings), Francis Dixon; George White; Dr Barnes; Mr T. Gardhouse Charlton and William Eggleston. Each tribunal also had a military representative, for Carlisle it was usually Major Fuller.

The first meeting of the Carlisle tribunal took place in the Town Hall on 24 February. The first issue to be decided was whether the press should be allowed to sit in and report the proceedings. It was decided that they should remain, unless an individual objected to their claim being heard in public. The appeals of early applicants were frequently dismissed: Clifford Vero, a photographer with no dependents who worked on his own and would have to close his business; an unemployed railway fireman who wanted to care for his mother; a boots at Graham's hotel appealed for a similar reason as did a man who was earning over £3 a week at Gretna. A monumental mason explained that he had lost three men out of six into the army. He had two brothers at the front and third had been sent back to work on the railways. He was appealing for another brother who worked for him. In dismissing the appeal the chairman commented that people wouldn't mind waiting longer for a tombstone.

The clerk to the Cumberland Insurance Committee was granted an exemption on condition that he remained in his present post. A part-time masseur who treated men in the local hospitals, but worked at Ferguson's mill, was described as being valuable to the medical service; he too was granted a conditional exemption. A projectionist at the Stanley Hall and Star Hall picture houses had his call-up deferred until 31 March as was that of the son of Thomas Graham, iron and steel merchant. The same decision was made in the case of the cashier and manager of the County Garage which had already lost seventeen of their twenty-four employees; their work for Gretna would be at risk if the man went.

Workers were given badges to show they were on essential work. Denis Perriam

The tram service was under pressure with the increased population. One of the council members suggested that instead of trying to run a service every ten minutes a reliable fifteen minute one would be preferable. Sir Benjamin Scott said that in war time people had to put up with inconvenience. Issues with the privately owned company running the service continued to exercise the council, writers to the press and the population in general throughout the war.

The Post Office moved from its site in Lowther Street to its new home in Warwick Road. Hospital trains passed regularly through the station and the injured soldiers were given refreshments. Local auxiliary hospitals cared for their patients and members of the public helped by providing treats and taking the men out to the country, or for tea. On 6 February 165 men, most with homes in Scotland and a few from northern England, arrived on a hospital train. The transfer to hospital was completed in an hour and a half, in spite of the lighting restrictions making the work more difficult.

The first married men were called up in early March because more men than expected had been granted temporary exemptions. There were still a large number of single men who had not been attested and steps were proposed to call them to recruiting offices and treat those who failed to attend as deserters. Adverts appeared in the Carlisle papers looking for female solderers at Hudson Scott and as packers and porters at Robinsons.

The air raid precautions were put in place in Carlisle for the first time. The alarm hooter at the gas works could not be heard by most of the population although the dimming of the lights was a good warning. The regulations also required people pushing prams to light them and cyclists had to display lights. The first case of a cyclist riding without lights brought before the Carlisle magistrates resulted in a fine of 40s and costs.

The widows of the driver and fireman of the troop train in the Quintinshill crash attended court to arrange for the investing of the compensation paid by the Caledonian Railway Company. Mrs Scott, left with six children of working age, but also two below the age of sixteen had been awarded £300, plus £10 a year for each of the younger children until they reached sixteen years of age. Mrs Hannah, left with a son aged six, received £270. The arrangements made by the judge gave each woman a weekly income and an allowance for each of the children to take them to working age.

Humour of the period; or is it encouraging recruitment? John Hughes

As the call-up of men in groups according to age and marital status continued so the tribunals became busy with men applying for deferment or presenting themselves as conscientious objectors who for religious or moral reasons were unwilling to serve in the army. The authorities had to decide how to deal with these men. A proposal to establish a Non-Combatant Corps which would not give the men military training but would use them for digging and other work not involving fighting was criticised by some in parliament. The celebrated case of Scott Duckers has been mentioned earlier but he was not the only man from Carlisle and the immediate area who took this course of action. The divide between married and single men widened and one correspondent to the *Journal* suggested that the Citizens' League might begin another Roll, but this one of 'Dishonour' or 'Roll of Shirkers'. People could add names to a list outside the League's offices and the individuals named could present any evidence to the League to defend their position and, if proved, have their names removed; no list appeared.

Those who were refused permission for extension or being excused from service at a local tribunal could appeal to a county tribunal which would review and reconsider the evidence. The one covering Cumberland and Westmorland had Sir Benjamin Scott, Mr J.C. Dove,

A detachment of Border men remained at the Racecourse, this picture was taken on 24 March 1916. Ashley Kendall

Ernest Lowthian and Joseph Chance representing the city among its twenty members. Cases dealt with by the county tribunal in early March included an appeal by an upholsterer who said that he had contracts to finish and needed time to deal with his accounts and affairs; the tribunal allowed him exemption until 3 April. A second case involved William Dixon, a grocer with a shop in Peter Street. He was a partner in the business with his father who was sixty-five and handicapped because of an accident nine years before; they used to employ an assistant and a carter. The assistant joined the Lonsdale Battalion and the carter also enlisted. In consequence Mr Dixon was doing all the work involved in the business, he was the only able man in the shop. Major Hope Brown, the military representative to the tribunal immediately withdrew his objection to the appeal as he now realised that as a food supplier Mr Dixon was in a certified occupation.

Two conscientious objectors were examined by the Carlisle military tribunal on 21 March. William Scott, a taxi driver, said that he refused to be the hired assassin of capitalist thieves, adding that he was incapable of physical work. When questioned he said he was not prepared to kill:

'The Mayor – Would you consider yourself justified in killing a wild Hun who had got hold of your mother or sister?'
Scott – 'I don't believe those tales about the Huns'
The Mayor – 'You would prefer that they be killed?'
Scott – 'I would reason with them.'
The Mayor – 'Suppose it was your life or his. Would you consider yourself justified in taking his?'
Scott – 'No I would not.'
The Mayor – 'You know we are at war? If there were a large number of gentlemen of your way of thinking we should lose the war'.
Scott – 'There would not be any war at all.'
The Mayor – 'You have read about what has taken place?'
Scott – 'I do not believe it.'
The Mayor – 'If we should lose this war is that quite a matter of indifference to you?'
Scott – 'Quite indifferent; I have no country to defend. I would leave it if I had the chance. The people who started the war should defend the country.'
The Mayor – 'Suppose one of our soldiers were badly hurt would you assist him?'
Scott – 'I would not help him.'
The Mayor – 'I have nothing more to ask you.'
Major Fuller – 'How do you think freedom of conscience has been won by Englishmen?'
Scott – 'It is not my fault I am an Englishman.'
Major Fuller – 'How was the freedom obtained?'
Scott – 'It has always been there.'
Major Fuller – 'You ought to be in a lunatic asylum. He is not much use anywhere else'.
Scott – 'That is a cheap sneer. You are very fond of cheap sneers.'
After the applicant had withdrawn the Mayor asked: 'Is he worth having?'

Major Fuller – 'No he is not worth having.'
Town Clerk – 'It was not a conscientious objection.'
The appeal was disallowed.'

The second case, that of Arthur Kippax, a labourer who was working on the erection of huts for workers at Gretna, expressed the view that he should not serve because he refused to commit murder at the bidding of another person. He said he had been opposed to militarism for twelve years and was an anarchist and free-thinker. He told the Mayor that he did not object to taking animal life; if a wild animal was attacking his mother or sister he would feel justified in killing it.

'The Mayor – Suppose it was a German?'
Kippax –' I would use my power.'
The Mayor – 'Suppose your power was not sufficient?'
Kippax – 'My mother would not want me to kill.'
The Mayor – 'She would prefer to be killed?'
Kippax – 'I would protect if possible but not at the cost of taking a life.'
The Mayor – 'Is it a matter of indifference to you who wins the war?'
Kippax – 'Well partly, I believe the war has been caused through financiers and diplomats.'
The Mayor – 'Never mind what it is caused by. Is it a matter of indifference whether we or the Germans win?'
Kippax – 'I don't think it will make much difference as far as the world is concerned.'
The Mayor – 'Are you an Englishman?'
Kippax – 'I suppose I am.'
The Mayor – 'You have lived here under the protection of the laws.'
Kippax – 'What do you mean by the protection of the laws?'
The Mayor – 'You are here in safety and comfort while others are risking their lives.'
Kippax – 'They believe in it, I object to it.'
The Mayor – 'Do your scruples go so far that you would not succour a soldier who was wounded?'
Kippax – 'I would be doing it voluntarily not through compulsion.'
The Town Clerk – 'It is the compulsion you object to?'
Kippax – 'Certainly.'

The Town Clerk – 'You are working at Dornock constructing houses for munitions workers.'
Kippax – 'Houses for the labouring classes to live in.'
In reply to the Mayor, Kippax said he objected to making munitions but not to building homes for munitions workers to live in.
Mr Eggleston – 'He says he is an anarchist. What is your definition of anarchism?'
Kippax – 'It is the abolition of law. Moral law is only law I admit.'
Town Clerk – 'Suppose there is nobody professing law but yourself?'
Kippax – 'I am not responsible for those persons.'
Town Clerk – 'They would not feel responsible for you for very long.'
The appeal was disallowed.'

More conscientious objectors appeared at the tribunal on 24 March. The only one who was successful in his appeal was Seymour Hutchinson, a chemist and bake house manager for Carr's. Both Carr's and Mr Hutchinson had appealed, on slightly different grounds; Carr's wanted to keep him working for them as they felt he was an essential employee. Mr Hutchinson was a Quaker who had long held religious objections to joining the army. In reply to questions from the Town Clerk Mr Hutchinson said that he was quite happy to know that some of Carr's biscuits went to the army as he had no objection to feeding soldiers.

'Hutchinson – I feel that all war is entirely contrary to the spirit of the New Testament and it is on those grounds that I could not take part in an army whose sole intention is to wage war.'
The Mayor – 'I take it that it is to the combatant service you object to?'
Hutchinson – 'Any service in an army whose sole purpose is war.'
The Mayor – 'Would you object to assisting wounded soldiers?'
Hutchinson – 'Certainly not. I was exceedingly anxious in the early part of the war to join the Friends Ambulance unit serving at the Front. On three separate occasions I put the matter before my employers they considered I was more necessary to the work here.'

> *The Mayor – ' In the present emergency what service would you render?'*
> *Hutchinson – 'I am willing to join the Ambulance Unit, I have no conscientious objection to ambulance service.'*
> *Major Fuller – 'Do you belong to the Society of Friends?'*
> *Hutchinson – 'I do.'*
> *The applicant was ordered for non-combatant service.'*

Both Scott and Kippax appealed to the County Tribunal that met in early April. Both cases were dealt with quickly and the appeals dismissed. Carr's also appealed for Hutchinson, but they were refused.

One man who had appeared at the first Carlisle Tribunal in February, Clifford Vero, a self-employed photographer, wrote to Major Fuller who passed it to the *Journal.* This letter from Sapper Vero of the Royal Engineers, thanking the tribunal for having made the decision to join the army for him.

The Reverend Bramwell Evans' services at the Picture House were increasingly popular. On 19 March the cinema was full, and over half the audience was male, mostly men from Gretna. It was announced that if the weather was inclement on the day of the next service the doors would open before the published time of 7.30pm. The Gretna men would appreciate this as many were turned out of their lodgings in the morning, work was closed on Sunday and the public houses were shut so they had few places to go to keep warm and dry.

The latest shortage to hit the country was that of paper because the government introduced a one third restriction to imports. Efforts to collect waste paper and card had been introduced in some areas and the government urged other local authorities and private companies, to follow suit. The local papers economised by reducing the long lists of names of donors and benefactors, but the lists of those killed and wounded continued to appear and grew longer. The city council dispensed with detailed reports and pages of accounts and instead provided members with summary reports on which they could base their decisions.

The Lighting Order was imposed on Carlisle on 14 April. As a warning to the citizens the papers gave examples from elsewhere in the country. Hotel keepers in the Borders had been fined because guests failed to draw the blinds. In Middlesbrough one man was prosecuted because he left a bonfire to die down as it got dark. Blinds at windows were often ill-fitting, leaving gaps at the side, and venetian blinds, unless fully closed, allowed light to be seen outside.

The order led to a flurry of correspondence in the press. People complained of walking into lamp posts, falling off kerbs and being unable to see bicycles approach. Solutions which were suggested included painting a white band around lamp posts about 5ft above the pavement, marking kerb edges with light paint and shading bicycle lights.

Other action to mitigate the dangers of air raids was instigated by Mr Robert Chance who offered to establish an air raid ambulance service, beginning by collecting volunteers with first aid training in the Denton Holme area.

The medical profession of the city was shocked by the death of Dr James Bird, at the age of forty-seven which was announced on 25 April. He had been one of the doctors frequently involved in work in the city and had helped at Quintinshill. His main work was in practice in Carlisle, as physician at the Infirmary and as secretary for the TB hospital at Blencathra. He had been ill for a fortnight, suffering from influenza but despite the best efforts of his colleagues and advice from specialists in Edinburgh he could not be saved. He left a widow and three children, the youngest aged ten.

The danger of invasion, coupled with the strengthened Aliens Act, and possibly some spite, led to accusations that certain individuals were of German extraction. During the war this happened on more than one occasion, the first recorded in the *Journal* was that of Mr Charles Padel, who since 1912 had been headmaster of the Boys' Grammar School. He was moved to write to the press to refute in some detail the allegation. Whether the assertion and rumour was started by a disgruntled student or because Padel was young enough at forty-two to volunteer was never made known, but he dealt with both in his letter. He described his parentage, a Danish father and part-German mother, who had lived in England for fifty years and had few German relatives. Padel had been born and raised in York where his father was a professor of music, had attended Cambridge University and spent his life in teaching. Although he had once admired aspects of German culture he had never liked the militaristic aspect of the country and he mentioned a former student who had reminded him of a warning he had given about the danger of German militarism and ambition in 1911. He had remained in his post at the school as he thought this was the best service that he could render his country. The accusation was not repeated.

The last week of April 1916 saw events which served as a backdrop to the summer in Carlisle. The sinking of a German ship carrying arms to Ireland and the capture of Sir Roger Casement who was associated with the 'Easter Rising' of Sinn Fein in Dublin, which in the view of many in England was instigated and certainly supported by Germany. This led locally to suspicions about the many Irish labourers who had arrived to work at Gretna. Also in that week parliament met in secret to discuss the recruiting question.

Some previously law-abiding citizens were brought before the magistrates on 12 May. The Lighting Order made it illegal to show a light at night and blinds and curtains had to be fitted. Among those who pleaded guilty and were fined five shillings was Canon Campbell, who lived in The Abbey, also his near neighbour the Reverend Stones who lived at West Walls. Richard Steele, a solicitor more used to being on the other side of the dock, was also fined as was the manager of the City Picture House.

The disturbances in Ireland, the frequent Zeppelin raids and hit-and-run raids by German ships on the ports of the east and south led those in authority to consider again ways to defend the area should there be an invasion. There had been attempts earlier in the war to raise a corps made up of older men prepared to undertake home defence. A meeting was called to attempt to raise two companies, a total of 500 men, from the Carlisle area. The list of those attending was a who's who of the city; the Mayor led the meeting accompanied by Frederick Chance, who was president of the Carlisle Volunteer Force, with his son Robert who at the age of thirty-one was judged to be unfit for the army but was adjutant of the Force. The need was great and the speakers were confident that a trained band of men could do much to serve the needs of the area. The meeting decided to support a resolution calling for the raising of a volunteer force in the city.

The introduction of the new Summer Time in May was not universally popular. Some farmers claimed that the fields would be still dew covered and so harvesting would not be possible. Others said that children would have less sleep before going to school. The fact that farmers had never been controlled by the clock and that the children would be into bed an hour sooner had to be explained.

At the end of May the government took the inevitable decision that every able-bodied man between the ages of eighteen and forty-one should be called up for war service. Attempts to operate a volunteer army had met with some success early in the war, but the mounting losses and slow rate of volunteering put the army at risk of having too few men. The Derby Scheme was a well-intentioned process which attempted to be fair in that it tried to protect men in skilled and *essential* trades, took first the men who were single and protected for a time those who were married. The organisation to keep the system moving, through the processes of registration, appeal and then county appeal was time consuming and of necessity could not be moderated across the country so anomalies grew. The soldiers at the front, particularly those who had volunteered in 1914, were increasingly frustrated with the 'shirkers' and welcomed the introduction of full conscription.

The War Office met with farmers' representatives to try to avoid the difficulties of the labour shortage of 1915. The annual Spring Hirings were almost non-existent because the shortage of available labour meant many farmers kept on the workers they had, although a few complained that men were asking for higher wages to stay. Workers were reluctant to move to other farms even for higher wages as they did not know if their exemption for service would be supported or as strong in a new position.

The call of the army for men between eighteen and forty-one meant that those either outside of the age limits or exempted because they were essential in their present positions or for medical reasons were in demand. Experienced men could easily get between £30 and £35 for the period to Martinmas in early November. The rates for boys too young to serve in the army were between £10 and £28 depending on their age and level of experience; an increase from the £9 to £12 of 1915. The rates for girls and women varied between £9 for a young girl just starting out to £17 for those with experience.

The War Agriculture committees were very aware of the shortage of labour and made efforts to find more volunteers willing to undertake farm work. Lists were created of young boys and women prepared to help. Schools were asked to encourage children to help in holiday times. This conflict between town and country continued with farmers feeling caught between the demand for increased food production, which included the change to more intensive grain and food production rather than livestock, and that for men for the army.

One aspect of the Hirings welcomed by the citizens was the accompanying fair on the Sands. The crowds were swelled by workers from Gretna and they were entertained by a range of stalls and rides. A menagerie, donkey rides, hoop-la, aunt sally, and coconut shies proved popular. A reporter from the *Journal* noted the number of recruits to the Volunteers who were trying their skill at shooting glass balls from jets of water. Although there was a thunderstorm in the afternoon many managed to change in time to get to the traditional evening dance at the Albert Hall. Many of those who weren't among the 500 to get to the dance went to one of the pubs in the city. There were reports of crowds lining up at the bars waiting to be served and at least one case of a pub closing early because it had sold all its stock.

Described by the press as the final fling of public houses under private ownership, the amount of drunkenness seen on the streets was the worst ever witnessed. A change that had been foreshadowed for some time was that of the take over by the Control Board of all public houses in the city. The intention of the order published in early June was that the board would take over and manage the four breweries and 119 public houses and impose controls on the sale of alcohol through clubs and off licences. Not only were 119 public houses too many for a city the size of Carlisle, counting only its peacetime population of 50,000, but many of them were in a poor state of repair. The tradition of men-only drinking houses was to be challenged and the requirement for public houses to provide food and non-alcoholic beverages like tea and coffee would encourage less alcohol consumption and make the pubs more welcoming to women. The licensed victuallers set up a group to meet the board when they came to the city.

The traditional two-day Whitsun holidays were cancelled in 1916 in Carlisle. The city council suggested that other companies might patriotically follow suit and so shops, offices and banks all stayed open as did the local schools. Not many people took a day trip and the coast and Lake District saw few people over and above the local populace.

Although surrounded by open countryside, parts of the city suffered pollution. The smoke from factories and an atmosphere polluted by chemicals resulted in an above average death rate. Even worse was the

Pratchitts in Denton Holme was one of the established engineering firms in the city that diversified into shell making. Ashley Kendall

Workers at Pratchitts gave up their Whitsun holiday. Ashley Kendall

rise in the infant mortality rate which at 133 per thousand in comparison with the national figure of 110 caused great concern to the Health Committee. The highest rate for fifty years, it was partly ascribed to outbreaks of scarlet fever and diphtheria. The death rate, accompanied by a comparatively low birth rate, was made worse by the death in 1915 of 172 infants before their first birthday. In consequence, and given the potential loss of men through the conflict, there was real concern that the fall in population would cause an economic decline in years to come.

The Carlisle Day Nursery was one attempt to improve the care of infants, particularly the increasing number of those whose mothers were working. At its meeting on 13 June the Council agreed to the appointment of two nurses and health visitors to work specifically with expectant mothers and infants. Earlier attempts to find suitably qualified women to do the work had failed and the Town Clerk was asked to ensure that candidates were qualified nurses and midwives, aged between twenty-five and thirty-five who could suggest their own wage rate.

Losses among local servicemen continued and equally worrying was the increasing length of the lists of wounded. The city was already becoming aware of the needs of men coming back and looking for work. The City Council on 13 June met the requirement to establish a committee to administer the War Pensions Fund through which payments would be made to soldiers, sailors and their dependants. This was another committee demanding the time of the Mayor, Theodore Carr, Mr Buck, Sir Benjamin Scott, Major Ferguson, Miss Henderson, Miss Creighton and Mrs Buchanan. There were in total, twenty-two members as the papers reported 'representing the council, the local tribunal, labour, the soldiers and sailors help society, and four women'. Those likely to be most closely interested, the working class men who formed the bulk of the servicemen, would, the Town Clerk assured the council, be represented on the sub-committees which would do most of the work.

News of Carlisle men with the services was published each week. Graphic accounts of shelling, gas, trenches and the experiences of marching, watching the enemy through periscopes and keeping clear of snipers gave the readers at home a picture of what the men at the front were experiencing. Photographs appeared of men who were wounded, others who won medals and those who had been killed. A particularly poignant pair of pictures recorded the deaths of Gladstone and James Burnett whose mother lived in Bishop's Court, Princess Street. James, aged thirty-two, had signed on for the Border Regiment but when he died on 4 June was serving with the Airline (signalling) Section of the Royal Engineers in Mesopotamia. His younger brother, Gladstone was aged thirty when he was killed just seven days later serving with 12th Battalion of the Highland Light Infantry.

The increasingly regular passage of hospital trains through the station ensured that nobody was unaware of the human cost of the fierce conflict taking place in France and Belgium and on the North Sea. On 6 July the Bishop of Carlisle received a telegram from Southampton to say that his 27-year-old son, Major Percy Diggle, an officer with the Lonsdales, was one of eight officers on a hospital train due to pass through Carlisle; he was recovering well after receiving a bullet wound through his shoulder.

The attack on the Somme on 1 July was the first major battle to involve the Lonsdales. In common with many New Army battalions they had worked in sectors of the front where, although there were regular losses because of random shelling, snipers and occasional forays into no man's land, they had not taken part in a set-piece battle.

They were in the thick of the advance on the morning of 1 July and by the evening according an eyewitness report had lost 700 of their original 1,000 men, killed and wounded. On that day 180 officers and men were killed including Colonel Machell. A full report of the battle did not appear in Carlisle until 11 July, by which time many homes had been informed of the death of a loved one. Of the dead ninety had enlisted in Carlisle, and forty of these had been born in the city.

This first report indicated that, like Major Diggle, other officers had been wounded including Colonel Machell and, specifically it mentioned Lieutenant Hodgkinson, a member of Carlisle Rugby Club who was commissioned from the ranks. One account from a man's letter was headlined 'THRILLING STORIES OF THE BATTLE', 'NIGHT IN A SHELLED WOOD', 'HAVOC BY MACHINE GUNS'. The same issue of the paper carried the story of the death of the colonel and how many of the men advanced singing the song *D'ye ken John Peel.*

Gretna Tavern, Carlisle, opened by Lord Lonsdale, July 1916. Ashley Kendall

The day after the details of the Lonsdale's losses were published Lord Lonsdale mentioned the tragedy that had come to Carlisle and the counties when he opened the Gretna Tavern and Coffee House in Lowther Street. The Control Board had taken over the old post office building, transformed it into a bar and restaurant and members of the Central Board from London were present to witness the occasion. The old sorting office was now a coffee house with tables and chairs for about 100 people. The dark-stained tables were covered in thin linoleum to protect the surface and the matching chairs bore the Royal cipher, 'GRI' in green letters under a crown. Speakers affirmed the purpose of the tavern as being a place where, rather than drinking in poor surroundings for the sole purpose of getting drunk, men and women could enjoy a drink, either alcoholic or non-alcoholic in pleasant surroundings and if they chose, have something to eat. The city's reputation as a centre for drink and drunkenness had to be removed and the Control Board was, in the view of many present, the way to ensure that the amount of drinking was limited to within controlled hours and in good buildings.

Normal civic life continued with the council dealing with the increasing cost of gas and electricity production. They were unable to order enough coal as the mine owners would not release it, the price of oil was estimated to be doubling and they had to pay allowances to men who had joined the army. The price of gas was increased by fourteen per cent. The 154 consumers of electricity were more fortunate because, although there had been an increase in costs, the company felt they could maintain the present price. Some members were at pains to point out that this was because of the lighting restrictions and the summer time act which meant more work could be done in the available daylight. The number of men in the Volunteer Corps was swelled not only by those given exemption by the tribunals. Others had joined and the corps in Carlisle had 450 members who paraded on Tuesday and Wednesday and, to allow those who worked, also on a Friday.

Specialists were also enrolled, a first aid detachment from the Carlisle St John's Ambulance and a motor cycle section comprised members of the Cumberland Motor Cycle Club.

The news from France in the middle of July was printed under triumphant headlines. 'HEAVY GERMAN ATTACKS REPELLED',

Morton Sundour platoon of the Volunteer Force. Ashley Kendall

ENEMY'S GREAT LOSSES'. The reports spoke of the capture of Contalmaison and Trônes Wood, and other key positions which the ordinary soldier could not have written about in his letters. Reports quoting letters from men in the Lonsdale Battalion told of men wounded and killed in the Somme action. One, who had been wounded twice before, was 18-year-old Thomas Strong, son of John Strong, a fishing tackle maker of Castle Street. Happily, both he and his younger brother, who was also serving with the Border Regiment, survived the war. James Harkness, before the war a promising footballer who played for Carlisle United and had captained his battalion football team, had a leg amputated. The Brown family, who lived at 66 Wigton Road, had already lost one son, Thomas, on 9 August 1915 in the Gallipoli campaign. They now received news that their other two sons were wounded and a nephew, Thomas Warbrick, had been killed fighting with the Lonsdales on 1 July.

The *Journal* of 18 July told of further Allied advances and victories. The lists of wounded from the Border action on 1 July continued to fill two or more columns of the paper so home morale, while being boosted by stories of advances and the taking of guns and prisoners, must have been affected by the local losses, even if the scale of total losses by the advancing Allies was not yet fully appreciated in the city. It was not just the men of the Lonsdales who had fought and died on 1 July. Private William Ferguson who had served in the Boer War and as a member of the Reserve returned to the colours in 1914 from his job as a brakesman on the railway, died with eighty-five other men from 2 Border. He left a widow and two children in Carlisle.

The darker side of life in the city was shown when Ruth Rafferty of Byron Street was sent to prison for three months with hard labour. The NSPCC had brought the prosecution because although the local inspector had tried to help the woman, described as idle and drunken who occasionally worked as a gardener, her four surviving children were dirty and verminous. Housing conditions generally in the city were increasingly under pressure and the growth in population and the unwillingness of the Ministry of Munitions to admit there was a problem and help the council was making the situation critical.

A change in routine which released VAD workers and saved money for the local Red Cross, was the decision by the military to provide hospital trains with sufficient food and drink for the whole journey to Scotland and thus end the use of Carlisle as a refreshment stop. So many men were now in hospital in Carlisle that the local VAD was

Casualties from the Somme were among patients in Murrell Hill House Hospital 14 July 1916. Ashley Kendall

finding it increasingly difficult to provide sufficient members to meet the trains at all hours of the day and night. In its final year between 1 January 1916 and when the service ended on 15 July, 7,198 casualties had been given food and drink at a cost to the local Red Cross of over £500, nearly £28,000 at today's prices.

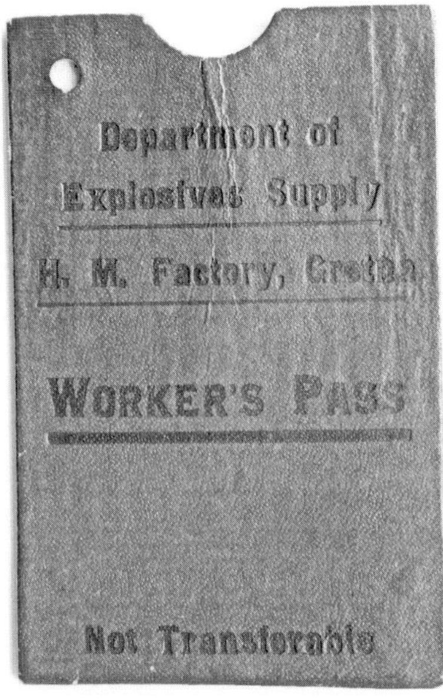

Jeanie Anderson's Gretna Pass. John Hughes

Jeanie Anderson and her younger sister Annie both worked in munitions but rather than live in the hostels at Gretna or Longtown they did the daily rail trip from their family home at 3 Tilbury Road, Botcherby. Annie also played football for a team of 'munitonettes'. The novelty of women playing football could guarantee a crowd for the increasingly frequent matches between teams from the various plants at Gretna, and also from Workington and Carlisle. The matches were all played to raise money for the Border Regiment PoW Fund, wounded soldiers and other charities. Clothing sometimes caused a problem. It was

Munitionettes football teams were popular fundraisers, East Cumberland Shell Factory Team, Carlisle. Ashley Kendall

claimed after one match that the losing team had been inhibited by the length of their skirts, the winners having shortened theirs to an unladylike length.

The summer meeting of the Women's Union listened to a talk by Miss Sandys of the Board of Trade about the work women were doing to support the war. Women, Miss Sandys told them, had taken on many of the jobs previously done by men in factories and munitions and on the farms. Objections by male factory owners and other workers were being overcome as the women demonstrated that they could work as quickly and to the same standard as men. Those opposed to the change, she said, argued that women and girls could continue to use their skills in cooking and house care and did not all have to become postmen or drivers to help the war.

Supervisory and welfare work in factories was of increasing importance as production had to be increased and many were working long hours. Mrs Chance spoke of the need to canvass the women of Carlisle to ensure that all were involved. Mothers with children could be supported because many of the members of the Women's Union were also on the committee running the expanded Abbey Street Day Nursery.

The union had also instigated the women's patrols in the city to ensure that women and girls were protected. The patrols were continued and there are reports in the press of the patrols and, later, women police becoming increasingly active in protecting and dealing with the workers from Gretna. Women police worked in the factory areas conducting searches to ensure no 'contraband', mainly matches and metal buttons, were taken into the danger areas. They patrolled the city, sometimes accompanying a male policeman, and travelled on the trains to ensure, not always successfully, that the girls remained in the 'women only' carriages. They also patrolled the women's hostels ensuring that the male visitors left by the 10pm curfew.

Another collection, this time for hospitals, realised £796 from the city, which was added to the sums collected from Cumberland (£378) and Westmorland (£48) to give a grand amount of £1,224, over £100 more

Badge worn by the Gretna police, female officers patrolled the trains to Carlisle. Mike Milbourn

than the total reached in 1915. The negative impact of over 10,000 working men living in close proximity to Carlisle continued to evince itself in the increase in drunkenness suffered by the citizens. Letters to the press only one month after the Control Board had taken over expressed surprise that the situation had not improved. The temperance movement was not reducing its continuing pressure for total abstinence. They were blaming the board, the Chief Constable, magistrates and the Watch Committee for the fact that there had not been an instantaneous reduction in drink-related offences. The Control Board, realising the scale of work required in the district, proposed to the local Watch Committees that it would split its operation and create a committee for the Scottish side of the border and a separate one for Carlisle, Longtown and north Cumberland. In contrast to this criticism the press congratulated the Control Board on the rapid fall in the number of cases of drunkenness in the city. From 11 June when there were forty-two convictions the numbers had gone down each week until 27 August when there were just eight. The local Carlisle and north Cumberland Board met for the first time on 6 September with Lord Lonsdale in the chair. Frederick Chance was elected chairman for subsequent meetings with Sir Robert Allison as vice chairman. After a brief review of the work of the Board since its inception the list of premises and firms to be taken over was agreed. It included the old established firm of Hope and Bendle in Lowther Street who had been providing off sales to the great and good of Carlisle for a century. The less well-established St Albans spirit stores and neighbouring Hole in the Wall were also taken as were the Queen's Brewery and public house in Caldewgate and the Friars' Tavern on Devonshire Street.

Juvenile crime continued to exercise the grown ups and at one meeting it was suggested that because young people were earning greater wages they were able to indulge themselves. One councillor suggested that the Chief Constable should ensure that ice cream parlours were patrolled. It was explained that while ice cream did not contain alcohol, the parlours did contain what he described as gambling devices and the opportunity to plan mischief, which could not be done when watching a film. Others were concerned that the examples seen in films could lead to bad behaviour so in all respects it was increasingly difficult for young people to do anything to please their elders.

The chairman of the munitions tribunal, the coroner and solicitor Thomas Strong, frequently appeared before the military tribunal on behalf of men appealing for exemption from call-up. At the military tribunal on 28 July he objected that one member of the tribunal had been reported in the press as saying that local solicitors seemed to be harbouring a number of young single men. The slander was exacerbated by the statement that many of these young men could be seen smoking round street corners. The Town Clerk said that he had not been present at the meeting but he could say that there were a number of young men smoking at street corners. The worker's representative, Mr Eggleston, agreed that he did ask how many of the men at street corners might be working for solicitors and this was picked up and reported; a journalist clearly saw a good story.

More positively the Citizens' League reported that since it opened the Soldiers and Sailors Rest Room in Court Square had catered for more than 20,000 men, 5,000 of whom had slept there. Money and other gifts continued to arrive at the League's office to support soldiers returning from the war too badly injured to undertake their previous work and in need of financial support.

The effect of the Lighting Regulation was considered by church councils during the autumn as the problem of blacking out the large windows would be difficult. Some decided to move the time of Evensong to mid-afternoon so that no artificial light would be needed. It would also be safer for the churchgoers to find their way home through the darkened streets. Some also thought an added benefit would be the removal of the excuse for young people to be walking together in the dark. They could have their walks in the afternoon instead, but those more realistic realised this might be a forlorn hope.

The military machine suffered from the volume of paperwork involved in attesting, calling up, medically examining and dealing with the appeals of thousands of men. One man was arrested in Carlisle as being a military absentee. David Lockerbie who lived in English Street had been attested but was temporarily put back on medical grounds having failed in his appeal in Liverpool. He had been called back but claimed he had not received the letter and was arrested. Another man, Henry Millard from Wiltshire, who was working at Gretna volunteered to join the Wiltshire Regiment and the army claimed he had been sent a rail warrant, which had apparently not arrived. Major Fryer told the court that in such an instance as this it was the responsibility of the man to report to the nearest recruiting office. He acknowledged that Millard's papers had been sent by mistake to Workington but were now in Carlisle. The magistrates decided in both cases not to impose a fine but to hand the men, who were not unwilling to join the army, over to the military. Less keen to serve, Patrick Maher a labourer, had been caught after a chase by police. He had refused to identify himself and answer questions from Colonel Ledward at the Castle, who told the court that under DORA this was an offence. The court agreed, fined Maher and handed him over to a military escort.

The court also dealt with the case of a Gretna inspector caught with a camera near the railway, an offence under DORA. John Yeardye lived in Margery Street, Carlisle and was an inspector of works at Gretna. He had been employed at Letchworth Garden City, one of the 'new towns' being used as a model for Gretna and advising on the work there. At the first hearing the magistrates remanded him on bail to allow the police time to have the film developed. When the case was resumed a few days later Yeardye's solicitor said that the case would depend on the interpretation of the Defence of the Realm Act. A private of the Royal Defence Corps, guarding the railway said in evidence that he saw the defendant with his camera but when he approached the camera was put down and a newspaper picked up. After he was questioned about having a camera and ordnance survey map in his possession Yeardye was arrested and taken to the Castle.

The Chief Constable explained that, under DORA, photography had been forbidden anywhere in the county, but on September 1 the area had been reduced to three specified districts where photography and sketching was permitted, but not if the pictures included military or railway structures. The defence solicitor pointed out that now the pictures had been printed none showed railway installations and his client was on a public footpath. His client had read the order to see where he could take pictures and had taken one of the Denton Holme waterfall and another of the market cross in Carlisle before he was arrested while walking along the river. The magistrates fined him 2 guineas (£2 2s) but the defence solicitor said he would appeal.

The losses and injuries suffered by men from the city and their families so far in the conflict encouraged the Citizens' League to take up the task of considering the opening of a workshop for wounded soldiers. One idea was to train the men to make things which before the war had been imported from Germany.

At the second meeting of the Local Control Board the matter of female representation had been addressed by the appointment of Ethel Sewell, the 34-year-old wife of a Stanwix solicitor as the first female representative. She had been in the city for six years originating from London. In addition the 69-year-old Miss Creighton, a well established city figure, and Louisa Carr, wife of Ernest and one of the large and influential family were appointed.

September brought the end of the harvest and many farm workers, who had been exempted until after that busy period, were due to report for army service. An attempt had been made to use soldiers to fill gaps where men had already gone to war, but some were judged to be of little help and farmers were reported as not being in favour of continuing the scheme, unless their own sons or nephews were enabled to return. Public schoolboys had arrived to camp in farming areas to assist but many of them arrived too late, although some farmers did compliment them on their hard work and willingness to help.

In late September the film of the Battle of the Somme arrived at the City Picture House and all showings were crowded as people tried to share what their sons and husbands had endured.

The control of the supply of sugar was managed by the government and in September 1916 there were complaints that too little was being made available for jam making, a staple provision in many homes and a way to preserve fruit. The shopkeepers were charged with limiting supplies and some decided to do this by only allowing shoppers to have a little sugar when buying a quantity of other items; a system unfair to those with limited money. A fairer system adopted in many Carlisle shops was to provide tickets to allow regular customers to buy sugar with other items. Petrol was also in short supply but the petrol control committee was hopeful in October 1916 that it would be able to release a little more for private use. Other shortages, notably in meat and milk were becoming evident and it was proposed that all non-manual workers should undertake to have a 'meat free' day to conserve the available supplies. Much of the meat supply was imported. The success of the German U-boat campaign was making huge inroads into imports of all kinds and although local famers kept

Carlisle well supplied, the picture in large cities across the country was less good.

Courts remained busy with an increased number of cases of drunkenness and child delinquency to deal with. Drunkenness was attributed in part to the poor housing in parts of the city and to the lack of resolution of the Control Board in closing down many small public houses in dark alleyways, which were difficult to police. The Lighting Order added to the volume of other cases, servants often blamed for failing to ensure that blinds were drawn, cyclists failing to have sufficient fuel for their lamps and gardeners whose autumn bonfires reignited during the night, in spite of efforts to dampen them down.

The brilliance of car headlights was problematic and drivers were ordered to mask the light allowing only a small amount to pass through a slit in an opaque shield. Later in October this allowance was removed and cars could run only on sidelights, or if they had candle or oil lamps. Shopkeepers were warned in October that they should not sell fireworks as Cumberland counted as a coastal county from which fireworks were banned.

Vehicles from Gretna added to the traffic in Carlisle, building materials and timber were frequent cargoes. D R Hampson

Cultural events continued with the opening by Lady Carlisle of an exhibition of paintings by local ladies. They were shown in Canon and Mrs Rawnsley's house in The Abbey. Between them the artists represented much of the city and surrounding district in their work, including some interiors of the Cathedral. The event raised about £90.

The October meeting of the Control Board agreed the purchase of more public houses in and around the city, and also announced that the sale of spirits for drinking off the premises would be limited to seventeen places in the city. This would replace the 107 public houses with full licences and five with off-licences which had been able to sell spirits previously. By the middle of October the board had closed thirteen public houses in Carlisle and taken over seventy-three more, leaving fifteen to be dealt with.

There was a proposal for a nationwide collection, organised locally by the *Journal*, to provide Christmas puddings for the troops. The army caterers had calculated that it cost 6d (2.5p) to provide a man with his ration; £21 would give enough for an infantry battalion. Although prisoners of war were not allowed to receive puddings the League was determined to open a collection to ensure that each man on their list of prisoners in Germany would get a Christmas parcel from Carlisle.

The farmers continued to receive criticism from those living in the city. One correspondent to the *Journal* pointed out that the price of bacon, mutton, butter, cheese, ham and eggs had all gone up by fifty per cent since the start of the war, milk had risen by sixty-six per cent. At the same time there had been no increase in the rates and rent paid by farmers, and 'most of their sons are still at home so all the profits are going into their pockets'. The writer compared this attitude to that of the members of the Citizens' League, the volunteers in hospitals, the VAD, the Volunteer Force and the sacrifice of the women whose husbands were fighting.

The supply of flour was becoming critical and the government took action to control the import and supply of grain. A leading manager of Carr's told the *Journal* that in their view the government had done the right thing in taking full control rather than trying to deal with parts of the supply.

On 12 October the Board of the Fusehill Workhouse met to consider a request for its use as a hospital. There had been a previous plan to use Fusehill but the military were now keen to take it on, along with

Brook Street and Norman Street Schools. It was hoped that there would be space in other schools to accommodate the pupils as the Education Committee wished to avoid half time working. The board agreed to contact the military to ask what timescale they had in mind to bring about the change. Other accommodation being considered for alternative uses were the hotels and other large buildings being viewed as possible hostels for girls working at Gretna.

Pygmalion, Bernard Shaw's romance, arrived in Carlisle in mid-October having opened in London to great acclaim in late 1914. The Her Majesty's Theatre was packed for the first night and it remained a great favourite for the whole of its week-long run. The Botchergate picture house advertised the arrival of a new shutter on the projector which, it claimed, made the films much more lifelike. The cinema was showing another episode in the Perils of Pauline an American series of twenty episodes each lasting between twenty and thirty minutes with each ending with a 'cliffhanger' to ensure the audience returned the following week for the sequel. At The City Picture House patrons could see Miss Fanny Ward in a film about Tennessee bandits. On 15 October the Botchergate picture house was again the popular venue for the Reverend Bramwell Evans' winter Sunday evening services.

The annual meeting of the Women's Temperance Association was an opportunity for Sir Robert Allison to talk about the Control Board in Carlisle of which he was the vice chairman. He indicated that while he was in favour of abolition and had hoped while an MP to pass some legislation banning Sunday drinking he thought the board was moving in the right direction to control drunkenness in the city. The Control Board had moved at some speed to take over and close public houses and remove licences from off sales grocers although two hotels, the Crown and Mitre and the County were not included in the board's plans.

The Border Coursing meeting was held near Longtown and a move to another field at Burnfoot-on-Esk allowed the supporters from Carlisle to arrive at the new station at Mossband, built to serve the works at Gretna and Longtown.

Price rises, reported in the press on 24 October when the cost of eggs in Carlisle market rose to 4d each and butter was being priced at 1s 7d or 1s 8d for a pound, prices not usually seen until January or February when supplies were naturally low. Lard, an essential for cooking, was impossible to find with no local supplies and imports from America commanding what had been the price for local produce. Most worryingly, potatoes were two to three times the price they had been before the war and supplies were very short. The farmers, suppliers and traders sometimes found it difficult to sell all their stock, but generally people had little option but to pay the prices demanded, and workers from Gretna had enough money to purchase what they needed.

Juvenile crime again attracted the attention of the press when it reported a Home Office conference on the problem. Factors identified were less school discipline, darkened nights because of the lighting restrictions, smaller number of police on patrol, and the demoralising effect of cinema. The best solution, it was decided, was for communities to provide suitable alternative attractions to divert young people and especially boys, away from the cinema.

The tram company was finding it increasingly difficult to obtain male drivers and the service was suffering. A trial in another city where wounded soldiers had been taught to drive trams had, apparently, failed when the men were put onto the routes and found it impossible to deal with the stress of the job in the traffic. Women, said the report, would not be strong enough to carry out all the tasks associated with driving a tram. The committee members were split on the issue with Mr Dalton and some others wanting to try women as drivers. However, because there were steep gradients in Carlisle where a woman 'might lose her head and panic in an emergency' and the existing drivers found it dangerous enough in the tight streets of some parts of the city, the committee felt overall that they were right not to allow women drivers, although some did take the controls when accompanied by a man on the plate.

The city was shaken in October when two police officers were accused of robbing workmen from Gretna. Constables McSweeney and Sherwin stood trial for robbing one man of a purse containing over £11 and another man of a gold watch worth £10 and a purse containing £2. The case must have cast a shadow over an event the following week in the Silver Grill Restaurant when the Mayor entertained members of the city force to a meal and entertainment to express thanks for the hard work done by the police during the year.

Progress was made on transforming the Fusehill workhouse into a

440-bed military hospital when plans were published to re-house the 200 inmates who remained. Over fifty men and women and some sick patients would go to Whitehaven. Shap workhouse, which had been empty for some time, was to be reopened to take other cases. The two schools, at Brook Street and Newtown would be fitted out to take 200 wounded soldiers between them.

The Guardians had to set up a local clearing house for any new cases and suggested that they move the children who were housed at Harraby Hill to the workhouse at Shap to vacate that space to accommodate new cases until they could be transferred. The Board decided to retain the services of the existing overseer and his wife to move the children but to advertise for a new married couple to supervise them, but that no man eligible for military service should apply.

Other children who were not in the workhouse needed care and the school for mothers and new babies had been running for some ten years. This institution supported those mothers and their children who were experiencing difficulty and had been supported by public donation. In the maelstrom of calls for charitable support it had suffered a dip in income and the increased amount of work because of the disruption of traditional family life meant that it had to appoint a full time trained worker. The redoubtable Miss Creighton published a letter of appeal in the local press, asking for donations to be sent to the treasurer, Mrs Carr, wife of Frank Carr of the biscuit and flour milling family

Families were warned at the end of October that because of the failure of the Scottish potato crop prices were rising in some parts of the country, but not yet in Carlisle. The government introduced limitations on the amount of food served in hotels and restaurants to two courses if served before 6pm and three courses between 6 and 9.30pm.

One effect of the war, noted earlier, was the sudden ending of the supply of German made dyes for the clothing and soft furnishing trades. In 1914 the British Government allowed firms access to German patents registered in London; but German manufacturers were confident that it would take ten years for British firms to discover all the secrets. In December 1916 James Morton wrote a letter to the *Yorkshire Post* in which he described how his company had been making dyes since February 1915. He wrote the letter because a company called 'British Dyes' had announced with some flourish that it had at last managed to reproduce one colour, Indanthrene Blue. James Morton, with justifiable pride, said that not only had his chemists produced this colour but manufactured others which had been equally difficult to reproduce. He wrote that he had not made an announcement of the fact as he was not selling the dyes but had been supplying both the home and foreign, particularly the American, markets with cloth dyed using these colours for over a year. He now thought he owed it to his chemists to make the facts publically known now that others were claiming the credit.

A national event which began on 5 December was reported to the people of Carlisle on Friday the 8th. Mr Asquith had been struggling to hold onto power for some months but was seriously weakened by events abroad. A Liberal, he had been Prime Minister since 1908 and to encourage political harmony had established a coalition government in 1915. Events of the war, notably the Dardanelles campaign and the shell shortage of 1915 had seriously weakened his position and he was increasingly seen as indecisive. The final blow to his authority came when David Lloyd George suggested the establishment of a small cabinet committee to run the war, but this was not to include Asquith. He at first accepted the idea, then changed his mind, but by then it was too late to regain any position of authority. He had for some time been subject to what he described as 'a well organized and co-ordinated conspiracy by sections of the London press'. King George V called a conference of senior ministers and first asked Bonar Law if he could establish a government, but this was not possible. The king then had to bite the bullet and ask Lloyd George, whom he did not particularly like, to form an administration. Lloyd George worked with Bonar Law and Sir Edward Carson to form a government which they achieved by 7 December. The government was no longer a full coalition as the Liberals decided to have only limited membership of cabinet posts. They promised that they would not disrupt the work of government and would patriotically support the efforts being made by the country.

The transformation of Fusehill workhouse to a military hospital had implications for the Red Cross and the administration of all hospitals in the area. The military organised the movement of casualties through base hospitals in the regions; the 1st Western Base Hospital in

Fazakerley, Liverpool had been carrying out this function for the Western District since 1914; this role was transferred to Fusehill. Although the military sent the casualties it was the responsibility of the Red Cross region of the base hospital to provide the transport. Carlisle's promotion to a base hospital city meant that the local Red Cross would have to find an estimated £1,000 a year (£56,000 today) to provide transport for the 1,000 beds it was now controlling. Lady Lonsdale led the collection of donations and the Mayor took on the role of treasurer.

We reproduce a Christmas card which was received by a Carlisle gentleman from Mr. H. B. Molyneux, a member of the staff of Messrs. Hudson Scott and Sons, who was in Germany when the war broke out, and has since been interned at Ruhleben. The card, which was printed and published by the "Ruhleben Camp Magazine," was designed by Mr. Molyneux.

It was not only soldiers who were imprisoned in Germany.
Cumbrian Newspapers Ltd

The rail system had come under increasing strain with some lines recording a fifty per cent or more increase in traffic. Fares on long distance trains would increase by fifty per cent, but those travelling on 'national business' could request a cheaper rate. There would be no trains for sporting events and cheap tickets for market trains would no longer be available. Soldiers' weekend leave was to be curtailed to reduce the numbers travelling but there would be some support those engaged in voluntary work and for semi-private war organisations.

A small paragraph in the *Journal* of 12 December told readers that both signalmen who had been held responsible for the Quintinshill crash in May 1915 were to be released from prison in Scotland. At the trial in the previous September Tinsley had been sentenced to three years penal servitude, Meakin to eighteen months in prison; both had served fourteen months. Those judged responsible for the Quintinshill tragedy were, strange as it may seem, supported by their employer, though this may be explained by the theory of the authors of *The Quintinshill Conspiracy*. Tinsley's family had been living in Caledonian Railway property in Carlisle since the trial, his wife working in the Citadel station cloakroom. Tinsley himself was re-employed by the company as a lampman and later a porter at Citadel Station. Meakin was found employment as a second man in the guards van of goods trains. He later set up a coal company which failed and he got a job as a clerk at Gretna.

The *Journal* fund for puddings for the troops closed on 12 December. All parts of the city and county had been represented in the list of contributors and the collection had realised £550, enough to provide puddings for 26,000 men. Donations ranged from the £21, given by the Mayor, Citizens' League, Canon Rawnsley and other notable names, sufficient to provide for a whole battalion, down to 6d from children and those of limited means which would give one man a pudding.

The wellbeing of the city in wartime was the responsibility of the Health Committee which met to discuss the regulation of the Local Government Board with regard to the treatment and prevention of venereal disease. The disruption of communities and the mixing of young men and women in unusual social settings made sexual contact more available and conditions were enabling the disease to spread. Punishment in the army was harsh, with men losing leave. In Carlisle a scheme for treatment and control was proposed which would be covering the whole county, in co-operation with hospitals in Whitehaven and Workington. If the government accepted the scheme the council could recoup seventy-five per cent of the cost.

The Health Committee was in conflict with the Control Board over planning of new and refurbished public houses. The board, it was said, was ignoring the council's bye-laws on providing drainage and not filling in spaces behind dwelling houses. The Control Board claimed that as it was a government office with Crown immunity it was not subject to council regulation. The council members were careful to point out that they were not opposing the efforts of the Control Board but in their view it was ridiculous that the board was not adhering to the standards which were improving living conditions in the rest of the city.

Those described as 'aliens' and others suspected of having German associations were under increasing pressure. Mr Padel's dilemma was described earlier and on 19 December a legal notice in the paper announced that Richard Schwabe, described as a gut manufacturer, was denouncing his surname and was now to be called Richard Sinclair. Sinclair was the grandson of Amalie Voight who farmed near Kingstown, 27-years-old, working as a maker of sausage skins but he

Rubman changed his family name to Robson. Denis Perriam

had previously been a shorthand typist working in the city.

At the end of December the discussion among the Carlisle Board of Guardians provided another example of prejudice based on wrong assumptions, similar to the issue around the headmaster of the Boys Grammar school earlier in the year. Miss Gertrude Heinrich was appointed as matron to the Fusehill hospital and based on her name some Board members jumped to the conclusion that she was of German extraction and so unsuitable. The *Journal* was quick to point out that she had been born in Britain and her family were all French originating from Alsace. The debate had been heated with one member asserting that 'only people of English blood should look after a hospital for English soldiers'. In the end the committee agreed to the appointment by a majority of 11 votes to 7, but one member was admonished by the chairman for making an aside comment 'that he wished the nursing staff "good luck" in working with Miss Heinrich'.

The court was again busy imposing fines for the breach of orders and regulations. Two market traders were fined for selling underweight butter, a case the Chief Constable admitted was taking a severe line, the pack was under by one eighth of an ounce (3.6gm) but the price of butter was such that an example had to be made. Five cases involved the showing of lights included that of the deputy coroner, solicitor Francis Soal, who lived on Scotland Road and had a light showing from his house, Thomas Foster of Dalston was fined £1 1s for driving a car with unscreened lights. William Johnson from Wigton was fined £1 for working an unfit horse at West Walls and the horse's owner was fined £2. Two men were fined for dropping rubbish on the street and two others for leaving ash bins out, a hazard in the darkened streets.

Food shortages were becoming acute and the government issued an Order in Council which allowed councils to take over unoccupied land and allow individuals to use it for growing crops. The Education Committee was concerned that the demands of the war meant that only three girls and no boys had entered training as pupil teachers. The committee was worried that this would adversely affect the quality of education after the war.

Christmas celebrations were muted. The 40th annual Reeves tea for the elderly was held in Charlotte Street School where 300 people enjoyed the meal and entertainment. Christmas Day was cold and gloomy but some bands did carry out the traditional tour of the city playing carols joined by a few people but by no means the numbers seen in previous years. Attempts were made by the Control Board to limit the excesses of the Christmas of 1915. A decision was made on 20 December to ban the sale of spirits in the city over Christmas but no announcement was made until 22nd, when it was too late for people to get supplies stocked up. Later court appearances suggested that although twenty-four Gretna employees were fined for drunkenness over the holiday period the lack of spirits had reduced the numbers significantly. For those workers from Gretna who had not travelled home, and others, the Botchergate Picture House had a full programme of pictures on both Christmas Day and Boxing Day, when a new Charlie Chaplain film was shown. The programme at the cinema during the year reflected the changing population with more of the films appealing to a female audience with themes of love, loyalty and fidelity, or the lack of it, as well as some adventure stories and newsreels.

The year 1916 had been one of great change in Carlisle. The census of 1911 recorded just over 46,000 people living in the city. An estimated 10,000 labourers arrived in the area to build the works at Gretna. Although not all those who arrived actually lived in Carlisle most visited for recreation as this was very limited in the rural areas where the factory was located. An increase of this magnitude, nearly twenty-five per cent, had a huge impact not only on housing but also on transport, supplies of food, clothing and power. Local builders who before the war had depended on local contracts to build, adapt or repair houses were affected by the prohibition on private building work costing more than £500. Neither an individual householder, nor the council could get much building work done.

The number of drunkenness cases continued to rise. Throughout 1916 the quarterly figures showed increases, the quarter from January to March had 175 more cases than the equivalent period of 1915, the second quarter had 317 more cases and the third 164. From the middle of the year the Control Board gradually took over all the public houses and imposed restrictions on the type and strength of intoxicating drinks available. The board also imposed a requirement, which was not followed rigidly, that public houses should provide food and non-alcoholic beverages to encourage a more family atmosphere. The temperance movement was still very active and did not agree with all that the board did, but could not argue that it had failed in reducing the number of cases of drunkenness appearing in the courts. Although the local courts were busy it was noticeable that the County Quarter and City Sessions had much less business than in previous years as the amount of serious crime diminished because, it was suggested, many of those likely to offend were in the army or employed at Gretna.

The Derby scheme to recruit men to the army had failed and all men of military age were now liable for conscription. By the end of the year an estimated 4,000 men from the Carlisle area were in the services and the number remained at about this level, in spite of losses, until the end of the conflict. One consequence of this was that increasingly the jobs traditionally done by men were being done by women, although this was not always popular with employers or the unions. Many of the men of business in the city were fully engaged with not only their own work but sat on new tribunals and the magistrates' bench on many days in each week. Tribunals for appeals against conscription had been established and munitions tribunals could discipline workers or, rarely, allow them to transfer from work associated with war production.

Local factories and mills were fully employed, not just making war related materials. Ferguson's Holme Head works was making cotton cloth but its range of fine dress cotton and voile was in demand both at home and abroad and this trade continued to thrive. Buck's flannel material and shirts were also in demand at home by the army but the company continued to supply its overseas markets in Australia, South America and South Africa. Carricks hattery, although it managed to fulfil its orders, had found it difficult having to train women to carry out jobs traditionally done by men and adapt the firm to accept the new workforce into what was a traditionally male domain.

Carr's continued to produce biscuits, though as the supply of sugar began to run out the range became smaller and fewer sweet biscuits were made. The needs of the military in France and India more than replaced the loss in home trade and the company found it impossible to keep up with the demand as one third of the men employed left to

Carr's were not slow to use the events of the war for marketing. Cumbrian Newspapers Ltd

join the army and had to be replaced by female labour who, it was felt, were less able to carry out the skilled tasks involved. Carr's marketing reflected the story of the war producing, in order, the *Belgian, Tipperary,* the *Anzac* and the *Jutland* biscuits.

The list of casualties with connections to the city grew. The lists published during July were particularly painful as the Lonsdale Battalion had been decimated in the attack of 1 July and many local families had sons and husbands killed or wounded. Trains which in 1915 had stopped in the station with wounded men requiring refreshment on their way to hospitals in Scotland now pulled into number one platform of Citadel Station to be met by Red Cross and VAD members with cars, taxis and, later, ambulances, to transport them to hospital. These strangers were adopted by the citizens and food and other gifts were delivered regularly to the hospitals. Those with cars offered trips to the country while others put on concerts, all designed to make the men's stay in the city as pleasant as possible. The Citizens' League continued its work of co-ordinating and initiating efforts to improve the lives of soldiers and their dependants. They were constantly busy collecting clothes, providing for prisoners of war, arranging flag days and collections, supporting the work of officials involved in recruitment and, probably most importantly, running the rest rooms in Court Square to give shelter to soldiers travelling through and needing somewhere to shelter while waiting for connecting trains.

The year ended with a personal tragedy for one of those usually found supporting and encouraging others. Canon and Mrs Rawnsley had both been suffering from flu over Christmas and while the Canon recovered slowly Edith Rawnsley died on 31 December. Aged seventy-one she had been married to Canon Rawnsley for thirty-eight years and they had one son who was serving in the army. The press reports of her death universally praised what she had done for the church and described their married life as 'one of singular charm and happiness'. Her love of art not only enabled her to provide illustrations for her husband's books but she had been instrumental in founding the Keswick School of Art. She provided one of the pictures used in the railway adverts for the Lake District and was a keen supporter of the creation of the National Trust.

CHAPTER 6

1917: War Routines, Local Services

Mournful start to the year – Trams and women workers – Youth clubs open – Potato riots – Women workers from Gretna – Hunting and fishing – Food shortages worsen – More government control – National Service Scheme – Temperance movement and grain supplies – More military success but more local casualties – Carlisle and changes in education – Canadians arrive – The magistrates and ice cream parlours – Restrictions on restaurant food – Bishop of Barrow and women's suffrage – Plans for new houses – "Drunkenness in Carlisle" – The Royal Visit – Women wanted for the army – More women into industry – Complexity of food regulations – Chief Constable accused of 'being German' – Whitsun holiday reinstated – Jam makers in court – Food Control Committee established – The end of leaving certificates – Housing improvements – Citizens' League achievements – 'State control unfair to restaurants' – Tackling the teenage problem – More conflict with farmers – Chewing cordite.

The shell factory in the city and the huge munitions works at Gretna and Longtown brought thousands of workers into Carlisle. The railway was running about forty per cent more trains than before the war. Workers were much more controlled in where they could work and their freedom to change jobs or their ability to take action against their employers was limited. While union action was not illegal, the moral imperative to support the war effort tended to make disputes, when they occurred, short lived and there were few instances of unrest. Most firms were involved directly or indirectly in war production. Engineering companies made shell cases and parts for guns. Cotton and linen mills worked flat out making material for military uniforms and workers. Around the edges of the city farmers were being forced to work with fewer, and older, labourers to help them. Horses were still being taken to pull wagons in France, the demand for home produced food increased.

Not all workers at Gretna made munitions, this shows a fireman's badge. Mike Milbourn

The military representative at tribunals was, unashamedly, after every man he could get, regardless of the impact on anyone, or anything, else. Employers, the self-employed and farmers all desperately tried to get workers exempted or have their call-up delayed. The 'rules' under which the military tribunals worked were not precise and there were variations between tribunals in how they were interpreted. It was often only after appeal to the County or national tribunals that some cases were resolved.

The year began soberly, under wet skies and grey cloud. New Year's Day was on Sunday, with all the public houses closed and the Control Board's ban on the selling of spirits still in force. The success of the prohibition on spirits sales over the festive season led the Control Board to impose a permanent ban on Saturdays. Churches held fewer midnight services than usual because of the lighting restrictions, and for the same reason not many went to visit friends to carry on the old tradition of 'first footing'. There were no football matches or other sporting events during the day and most people who did venture out of doors went to one of the cinemas or the theatre.

The sombre mood continued on the 3rd when Mrs Edith Rawnsley was buried at Crosthwaite. Canon Rawnsley was not well enough to attend but their son Lieutenant Noel Rawnsley managed to get leave. The Bishop of Barrow took the funeral service. Lady Mabel Howard was assisted in her task as pall bearer by Mrs Chance and Mrs Buchanan and three other notable women of the district. At the same time as this service was being held there was a memorial service in Carlisle Cathedral attended by the Bishop of Carlisle, the Mayor and Mayoress with the Carrs, de Schmidt, Creighton, Henderson and Sewell families represented along with many of the local clergy of all denominations. The respect for the Rawnsleys was huge and extended across the whole of the district.

The usual pressures of life continued in the city. The tram service continued to be a cause of concern to the council and the courts. The Chief Constable asked that the tramway company be sent a letter which refused permission for them to employ women drivers. The courts fined the local manager and one of the men found driving a tram 10s each for driving without a licence. The man had been classed as C2, unfit for service, because he had poor eyesight.

War related cases continued to fill the magistrates' court. A Belgian, Julien Hyzeth, was fined for failing to register a change of address when he travelled from Carlisle to London to join the army, and that he had moved to a new address in Carlisle as required by the Aliens Act. Five drivers were fined £1 1s for failing to have the correct lights on their cars and six people were fined various amounts for showing lights, including the manager of the New Public Hall who had thirteen red lights shining outside his premises.

A tribunal heard an appeal from Morton Sundour in respect of a 19-year-old Mancunian, Sydney Dunworth. Major Hope-Brown, for the military argued that Dunworth was too young for exemption and as he had got a degree at an age when other young men were just entering university, he should be going to serve the army. Mortons said he was essential in doing the laboratory work essential to the development of dyes. The tribunal agreed to Dunworth being exempted from non-combatant service and be retained at Mortons.

Before beginning business on 9 January the City Council paid tribute to one of their members George Nichol who had been missing since 1 July but was now confirmed as having died. A laundry van man aged twenty-five he had been on the council for three years before joining the Lonsdales.

Normal business dealt with regular topics. The increased demand for electricity from the growing population and the demands of the munitions and other factories meant that consideration had to be given to purchasing spare generating machinery at a cost of £9,000. Land had to be found for food production and, while it was estimated that 1,000 allotments could be made available, the council instructed officers to look at all the land owned by the council to identify how much could be released.

On 11 January a girls' club was opened in the Kings Hall, Globe Lane. With financial support from the munitions committee of the YWCA and with a membership fee of 2d per week, it was intended to appeal to munitions workers, shop girls and domestic servants. There would be opportunities for dance, music and games and classes in ambulance work, cooking, musical drill and singing. A boys' club was also opened in the premises of the Boys' Brigade on Abbey Street to give access for boys on three nights in the week to a place where they could play games indoors, use the boxing facilities, and join in classes on boot mending, joinery and ambulance work.

The increasing price of food, particularly potatoes, led the Food Controller to impose maximum price, but sellers in markets at Maryport, Keswick and Carlisle tried to sell at higher. Housewives protested and in some cases refused to buy until the price was at the recommended level. Farmers and market traders who attempted to remove unsold potatoes from the markets were surrounded and threatened with violence. The riot in Carlisle on Saturday, 19 January began after some sellers arrived and began asking 2s a stone, later arrivals tried to sell at 1s 6d and had a few takers but when one trader asked 1s a stone he immediately got buyers who then chastised the ones asking more. The *Journal* recorded:

> *'A woman somewhat excitedly rushed to the top of the street and shouted "a shilling a stone or over goes your cart!" ... A crowd of people surrounded the carts and many epithets were hurled at the sellers and cries were heard of "a shilling a stone or we'll give you a bit of the Maryport do!" and "you want some of the miners wives here!" The price fell to 1s 6d and a man who had sold a few at 1s 10d was obliged to return the 4d. The farmer who sold at 1s promptly sold out. The temper of the crowd seemed dangerously high but the presence of policemen prevented any serious trouble.*
>
> *Inside the market things were quiet until a woman followed by a man rushed out and shouted "they are turning my cart over" and to the man "follow me if you dare". The cart was not overturned.*
>
> *Rumours persisted in the butter market that a disturbance would occur there unless prices were lowered but nothing happened'.*

At Maryport, where the disturbances had begun, farmers refused to attend the market to sell potatoes. However their wives who had tried to sell butter there were challenged about the price and while some carried their butter away, to jeers from the crowd, others sold at 1s 8d, a drop of 6d on the price being asked at the opening of the market. The farmers realised they would not get more and capitulated, the women buying as many potatoes as they could afford. At Keswick just two farmers arrived with potatoes. One woman put her hands on a farmer's cart and when he remonstrated with her soldiers on leave joined in and both carts were overturned to the delight of boys in the crowd who filled their caps and pockets with as many free potatoes as they could carry.

In Carlisle the following week housewives waited in vain for the arrival of farmers' carts into the potato market. The few potatoes available were eventually sold at 2s to 2s 4d a stone. The price remained high as sellers continued to boycott the market saying that until the government fixed the price they were not willing to sell their crop.

A dramatic raid on a jewellers shop in English Street excited and angered the readers of the local press in early February. Norman Grant aged thirty-one was the owner of the shop, but he had joined the army leaving his wife in charge assisted by two sisters and an older man who was a porter. The police suspected that the raiders were also responsible for a similar theft in Edinburgh, and there was much indignation that a man who had gone to war leaving women in charge of his business was targeted in such a theft.

The works at Gretna attracted huge numbers of women, many below the age of 20. Hostels were prepared using the Yeomanry Riding School, the adjoining Skating Rink, the Great Central Hotel and the Conservative Club. The facilities in the hostels and the girls' club were intended to keep the women and girls safe from the attentions of the thousands of unattached men. Some liaisons did take place. Reports from the women police who were recruited in February 1917 to work in the city and at Gretna recorded that men were fined for talking to the girls on the station platforms, which was against the rules.

The *Journal* of 2 February contained advice for farmers on ploughing and preparing land for potatoes, and gave the new price per ton of seed potatoes. Local allotment societies were set up at

Gretna Munitions workers. Ashley Kendall

Edentown and Stanwix. Another community meeting was called in the Town Hall to promote the buying of War Bonds. The Mayor was unwell, as was Mr Chance and Canon Rawnsley was still convalescent but most of the notable families in the city were represented. War Savings were encouraged and the challenge had been laid down by the national organiser that surely the British could do better than the Germans who had managed to raise £110million in their latest war loan campaign.

The Licensing Committee responded to the complaints of a number of people about the effect of cinema, and the associated posters, on the young of the city. They decided that no child below the age of six would be allowed in a cinema and re-imposed a rule which had been allowed to lapse that school age children going to the cinema after 9pm should be accompanied by their parents or a guardian.

The demands of military representatives on tribunals to get every able-bodied man into military service sat uncomfortably alongside the pressure being put on farmers to plough more land and plant crops with which they were unfamiliar. At one farmers' meeting it was suggested that if all Irishmen were sent to work on farms rather than to the military then farmers would be more willing to release men. At the present they were offered 'substitutes' to replace men taken for the army but these were 'tailors and clerks with no idea about farming'. The arguments became polarised and personal as many farmers protested at tribunals that to ask on one day for more land to be ploughed and on the next to take the ploughman for the army was not going to solve the food shortage. One military representative at a Carlisle tribunal was heard to comment about farmers' sons, 'they have kept the plums to the last'.

The lack of shop staff was causing queues and delays. To alleviate this the Carlisle Chamber of Trade asked the people to try to do their shopping during the week to allow those who lived in the country to have access on Saturday. They also opened a register to allow those above military age to offer their services for other aspects of national service on a part-time basis.

Hunting and fishing activities continued, some to alleviate the food shortage, but there were limitations. The opening of the fishing season was described as the worst for many years. Cold weather and ice on the water limited access to the Eden and Esk. A few salmon had been landed but the opportunities were few. Salmon netting in the Solway, which gave food for market, had been open but no boats had been out in the bad weather. The masters of foxhounds meeting in London proposed a reduction in the amount of hunting but this was not met with enthusiasm. Lord Lonsdale had already decided to meet all the expenses of the hunt at his home in Rutland. The local hunts published the dates for their first meets, and as 1917 progressed there were complaints from farmers that the more limited number of meets was resulting in a greater loss of stock from predation by foxes. Hare coursing was being affected by the building at Gretna which was on land traditionally used by the Border meet. The munitions board could ban coursing on land used for munitions, and had already taken this course of action in Durham but not yet in the north-west.

The Chief Constable's report to the city council referred to changes brought about by the war. Forty police officers were in the army and those remaining had been under great pressure because of the increased population but the 100 special constables who had volunteered for Sunday duty provided an opportunity for regular officers to have a day off. Women police were a new departure, many were deployed at Gretna but there was a permanent force in the city working from their offices in Portland Square to supervise the growing population of young female munitions workers. The major problem of drunkenness showed Carlisle in a poor light with an increase of 676 cases, but of the 953 convictions 788 were of people working at Gretna and another 47 were of strangers passing through; only 118 people with a permanent Carlisle address were convicted.

British and Allied raids during the winter had weakened the Germans and their counter-attacks were ineffectual. The stock of munitions had increased and preparations were being made for Allied offensives in the spring. Losses diminished but remained steady during the winter with men from Carlisle among the casualties, and the local hospitals remained full with regular arrivals of hospital trains.

Potato supplies and prices rose to the point where one trader managed to sell at 2s 9d for a stone, but the normal price was between 2s and 2s 6d. The War Cabinet met and set a price of one penny and a halfpenny per lb until 31 March and then a penny three-farthings giving a price of 1s 9d for a stone rising to 2 shillings and a halfpenny. Sellers were reluctant to sell at the new prices claiming that they had paid

An illustration from Reverend Stuart Wilson's book showing what he said were scenes he observed in Carlisle January 1917. Carlisle Library

more for their stock in the open market. It was not only potatoes; the control of the price of milk was to continue.

The effects of price rises and shortages were not just felt by the housewives. St Mary's Home had fallen into deficit at the bank, the matron of Murrell Hill was asking for people to donate potatoes as she did not have enough to feed the patients. In the poorhouses where the staple diet was based on bread and potatoes the high price of one and shortage of the other made things difficult. The food minister had suggested that individuals should limit their ration of bread to 4lbs a week, the average weekly consumption per person in the workhouse was 11lbs. Alternatives like beans and lentils were being used by some but were not a popular option. Price control did not ease the supply situation; on 27 February there were no potatoes offered in the market.

The Volunteer Force, with the task of defending the county in the event of a German invasion, was commanded by 32-year-old Major Robert Chance who was exempt from conscription on medical grounds. Volunteers were asked to offer themselves and any vehicles as 208 men were needed. There would be no payment for training, apart from the costs of petrol, but if the force was called to action then the normal military rates of pay would apply. Recruitment began again in January and continued throughout the year with Theodore Carr, commanding the transport section, writing letters to the press inviting more men to join the unit. Members of the Cumberland Motor Cycle Club offered motor cycles and others offered lorries and cars.

The Gretna Tavern was reported by the Control Board to be a great success with sales of food making up nearly seventy per cent of the taking. On Saturdays the Tavern sold about 200lb of cooked meat, forty stones of potatoes, sixteen gallons of soup and quantities of other food. Opening at 7.30am, men who had sleeping accommodation without food could get breakfast. An attempt to provide coffee carts for workers using the station was not successful partly because the Station Committee refused permission to have them under cover inside.

There was a flurry of official activity and instruction. The government announced that new orders would be placed to allow the Board of Agriculture to enforce food production. To free space on the reduced tonnage of shipping arriving in the country certain items were no longer to be imported. A partial ban was imposed on timber, paper and paper materials, oranges, bananas, grapes, almonds and nuts.

Farmers were to be offered £3 a quarter for wheat; oats £1 18s 6d; potatoes £6 per ton.

The national service scheme designed to get men and women into key industries had, by the middle of March, attracted 100,000 volunteers but Neville Chamberlain wanted five times as many. The government acknowledged that because of the lack of co-ordination between its departments it had been a mistake to strip men away from agriculture and important businesses. The scheme was failing in its task of managing the allocation between military and industry. Volunteers were asked to put their names forward if they were between the ages of eighteen and sixty.

The Board of Education came to an agreement with the military which would mean that teachers classed in category A or who had not been medically assessed, would be available for call-up. In return any teachers already in the services, but in category B1 would be released on condition that they returned to teaching. The unions were concerned that this would result in more unqualified teachers being employed in schools and in all probability more women would be employed in boys' schools. The employment of female teachers in place of men who had gone to war led to a demand from the National Union Teachers for equal pay. Women were paid less than male teachers, partly it was argued, because they usually taught younger children and girls.

The temperance movement meetings in the city attacked the use of grain, which was in short supply, being used for the production of beer. Robert Chance was a very vocal chairman claiming that not only would the ending of brewing save grain it would also release men for the services and end the absenteeism often experienced by companies on a Monday morning. It was accepted that there was a need to continue to make industrial alcohol but not to make drinking alcohol. Grain for food was far more vital than drink.

The reports of the progress of the war in March began with headlines proclaiming 'BRITISH ADVANCE ON THE ANCRE', 'OUR TROOPS WITHIN A MILE OF BAPAUME'. The papers continued to give details of men being killed and injured. Private Joseph Earl, whose parents lived in West Tower Street, died in a German hospital after being captured. A 30-year-old Carlisle man, Corporal Robert Castle serving with the Australians, died from wounds in France. He used to work at the Holme Head Works before leaving

From 'State Drunkenness in Carlisle' Reverend Stuart Wilson.
Carlisle Library

for Australia, but was expected to return to visit his family who were living in Norfolk Street, Denton Holme.

The drive to produce food locally in allotments and gardens was encouraging people to begin to prepare their plots, but they were not helped by the coldest February and March weather ever recorded in the city. Farmers were suffering similarly and the director-general of food production urged ploughmen to work from dawn to dusk to get the soil broken and ready for sowing.

There had been a national appeal for those who did not need to use potatoes to stop using them for three months. The Carlisle magistrates fined a trader, Mary Grice of Botchergate, for selling potatoes above the agreed price of 1s 9d for one stone. The magistrate fined her £1 and said that any repetition of the offence would attract a harsh punishment. In the market the traders were selling at the correct price and attempted to ration supplies. The *Journal* of 13 March described the scene:

> *'Pale faced and ill-clad children scrambled amid the crush and offered their string bags for their allotted amount. On one occasion one old lady scarcely able to walk received her potatoes into her apron. As she hobbled away she muttered "thank God I have been able to get these".'*

Trouble was avoided by two policemen who organised the crowd into a queue and made sure that nobody tried to get more than the allowance of 4lb for each person.

The vexed problem of education, which has affected every generation, was under the direction of local authorities, with the Board of Education setting government direction, but without having overall control of the local system. Herbert Fisher, who took over as Minister of Education, was in favour of more central control and direction. During 1917 the debates about education, and Fisher's Bill, showed the first glimmerings of society considering what might happen after the war. Carlisle was not slow in participating in the debates with Canon Rawnsley and others, as well as the teachers' associations, contributing ideas for the future.

The preparation of young people for adult life and work was seen as the necessary objective with a proposal that after the school leaving age was raised to fourteen there would be continuing education for all young people until they were eighteen. They would be open during working hours and an annual attendance of not fewer than 329 hours, equivalent to about forty-one days, was required. The additional expenditure of £6million was said to be equivalent to one day's military spending. This is one debate still unresolved one hundred years later.

The National Service scheme was launched in Carlisle on 9 March. The commissioner for the northern counties, Mr Lauder, described the work of local committees and said that they should represent all parts of the workforce. Men transferred to new employment would continue to get the rates of pay they enjoyed prior to transferring. Employers would have three days to appeal against losing a man, but once the tribunal had met and given a decision there would be no further appeals.

Sunday service in the Botchergate Cinema. The Reverend Bramwell Evans, Methodist minister wanted to provide something to keep the Gretna workers suitably entertained, and warm and dry, on Sunday evening. Denis Perriam

Men in uniform arrived in the district to take on specialist work. The Canadian Lumber Corps had been sent to the district to fell timber for the war effort. At a concert organised to welcome them to the city by the Fisher Street Presbyterian Church in West Tower Street Hall their commanding officer said that they were grateful for the welcome. The military was releasing ploughmen from military training to return to break the soil. The officer in charge of placing them expected a further 120 men, all originating from the counties. Other men, not skilled in farm work but capable of doing work under supervision had also been identified and put to work.

The coming of spring marked the last of the Botchergate Picture House services for the year. Mr Evans also collected money for a hut at Dornock, near Gretna, to serve as a base for social and religious work. He had raised £950 (£44,000 in 2012) and was hoping to achieve £1,200 (£55,000) by the last service on 1 April. He moved himself and his family into a hut nearby to continue his work. In the days before driving lessons and tests his wife reported some trepidation when they first set off in the little car he had obtained to allow him to move between Carlisle and Gretna. As a result of writing regular letters to the papers asking for help he found lodgings for about 1,000 Gretna workers.

As in the previous year there were problems with the ice cream parlours. Younger boys and girls found that the parlours were remaining open after the regulated shop closing time of 8pm. The owners claimed that they were able to do so because they were selling food. Over 100 young people crowded into one of the parlours to buy ice cream. Magistrates took a dim view of the claim that ice cream was food and the Chief Constable complained about the 'disorder' that resulted as the customers made their way home. Peter Ardriani (Pietro Adreani in 1914 Directory) whose parlour was in Scotch Street and Raffaells Turricchu were both fined £2 (£100 today) and warned that they should follow the order about closing at the correct time. It was made very clear to them that the magistrates disapproved of their actions, calling ice cream a luxury which was certainly not a food. Crowding together might also be a health risk as the city was experiencing an outbreak of measles, 396 of the population had succumbed to the disease, with eight of them taken to the isolation hospital.

News about the war was encouraging. The papers still had reports of casualties and portraits of men killed and wounded but the lists weren't as long as in 1916. The army still needed men and the creation of training battalions to cater for those aged 18 to 18 years 8 months were greeted positively as they could cater for the needs of younger recruits.

Older men were still sought by the army and one of the cases considered by the Military Appeals Tribunal was that of Alfred Body, manager of a boot shop in English Street. The original appeal heard by the city tribunal had exempted him from service on the grounds of hardship and the fact that his mother, who lived in Guernsey, was coming to live in Carlisle. The military representative appealed against this on the grounds that the tribunal should not consider his family circumstances, just whether the man was fit and not in essential work. In evidence to the appeal tribunal Mr Body's representative pointed out that his client was not selling boots he was repairing them and as nobody in Carlisle was able to buy new boots they all needed to have the ones they had repaired and there were few men around to do it. In addition a man from Mr Body's shop travelled to Gretna three times a week to pick up and deliver boots for repair, mainly from the women police. The tribunal dismissed the appeal from the military.

In April President Wilson, whose mother had been born in Carlisle, addressed the US Congress advising them to throw the weight of America behind the Allies. The press indicated that the American people were behind their President and were keen to send their reportedly well-trained and fresh soldiers to Europe. There was also the belief that America had ships, tanks and guns to send across, relieving pressure on Allied production. In the event the American troops arrived and bolstered the exhausted French and British armies but used British and French equipment to fight the battles.

More than 100 members of the Fusehill allotment association attended a social evening in the Co-operative Café. They were provided with a supper, an extensive concert and speeches praising the association and encouraging members to continue after the war.

The Mayor called a meeting at the Town Hall to discuss the food crisis, but it was poorly attended. The government was unwilling to impose rationing and was hoping that individuals might limit what they consumed to allow supplies to be shared out, and sent to the troops in France. Speakers were keen to offer ideas and support, but some were of the opinion that restrictions could only be successful if they were imposed centrally. The only thing that this meeting could do was try to persuade people to limit their intake of food to a level sufficient to keep them in good health. The proposed ration to follow was 4lbs of bread a week, 2½lb meat and 12oz of sugar, which the Mayor thought was adequate. It was proposed that the War Savings Committee, with help from teachers and insurance agents, who visited many homes each week collecting deposits, would spread the message. Women's meetings and guilds would also advise their members about feeding families.

Another regulation came into force limiting the amount of meat, sugar, bread and flour to be consumed in hotels and restaurants where the cost of a meal was above 1s 3d (£4.90p today). On days when meat was not served customers wanted to replace it with bread and viewed fish as a poor substitute. When meat was sold the quantities were smaller than before the order was imposed, but prices remained about the same.

Another indication that thoughts were moving to the period when there would be no war was the proposed electoral reforms set out by the Speakers Conference. At a meeting in Carlisle much of the emphasis was on the issue of women's suffrage. The Bishop of Barrow in perhaps a cynical tone declared himself to be a late convert to women's suffrage but went on:

> *'Don't let women ever think that men are not clever. By making the age limit 35 a woman has to choose between being 35, and having the vote, or not 35 and having no vote.'*

His concern in what he described as his unregenerate days was that women would be degraded by mixing with politicians but now his faith in politicians had sunk and he hoped that women might do a good deal of cleaning out in dark places in political life. He used to feel that women had not the balance for the political life but in their acceptance of a compromise seemed to 'establish a balance and commonsense which would have done credit to the warring factions in church and state in years past'. In social questions he hoped that women would prove to be a driving force and use their greater knowledge of social issues to influence parliament. Another speaker expressed the view that it was what women had done before the war that gave them the right to vote. What they had done during the war simply defeated any anti-suffragist arguments in a way no amount of talking could have achieved.

The YMCA opened another refreshment room in Fisher Street for the use of 'men in khaki and munitions workers'. Open every evening and staffed by ladies of the Carlisle YMCA ladies committee, the room would provide refreshments and a place to read and write letters.

The Health Committee discussed the plan for new houses for working families at Denton Holme and Boustead's Grassing. Alderman Dalton objected to the requirement that the houses be built with space around for garden allotments and described the board's inspector as a 'crank'. The Medical Officer said that in his opinion it would have been beneficial to the population if there were more such 'cranks'. More space around houses would have reduced the death rate and resulted in fewer delicate children. Although private landlords might want to have the maximum number of houses in a confined space the health effects were such that he was pleased that such reactionary practices were no longer permitted. The committee also discussed the allotments being created and it was suggested that they propose to the City Council that a prize or prizes be offered to encourage their development.

Reports in early May made it clear that the much publicised national service scheme was a failure. Most of those who registered were already in vital war work. The demand for soldiers was so great that munitions workers, unless they were engaged on really essential work, would now be 'combed out' to move from producing to firing shells.

An editorial in the *Journal* on 8 May 1917 reported the publication of a letter headed 'State Drunkenness at Carlisle' published by Reverend Wilson Stuart, a Methodist minister from Birmingham. His descriptions of the city, based on visits made between January and March are lurid accounts of drunkenness and behaviour accompanied by cartoon illustrations. His stories would, it was felt by the writer of the editorial, be popular with the drink trade, who were still complaining about the board, but did nothing for the temperance movement as the figures for drunkenness did not support Mr Wilson's account. The number of cases of drunkenness continued to fall; the figure for April 1917 was thirty-one compared with ninety-eight in the previous April. Over the coming months, although Mr Wilson visited

A scene reportedly observed in Carlisle, January 1917. Carlisle Library

Carlisle, he gained little meaningful support and was viewed as a trouble-making outsider doing little to contribute to life in the city.

Fiction mirrored fact in a play put on by the women police based at Gretna. The story line featured three woman all waiting for their boyfriend, or in one case, husband to return from the front. Acrimony ensued as they believed that they were all waiting for the same man. At a court in Carlisle a woman from West Cumberland was charged with bigamy which came to light when her husbands, one a soldier from the south of England, both turned up outside the post office where she worked to walk her home.

The differences about budget between the county and extended city were partly resolved when the City Council agreed to transfer £10,000 'without prejudice', to the county to meet the £80,000 losses claimed in rateable values. The city had also incurred costs of transfer, not least in the payments to the Grammar School. The final reckoning was taking some time to resolve and despite the war local issues continued to require the attention of the burghers of Carlisle.

Criticism of the government's action on food became more strident as the number of items in short supply increased. The suggestion that people should find substitutes for meat and wheat led to increased demand for direct substitutes. The reduction in bread was the most difficult to manage as the normal substitute would be potatoes, which were also in short supply. One local company trying to supply the demand for different sorts of foodstuffs was Carr's. They were advertising their biscuits as providers of instant meals for the busy housewife and working mother. The sugar content of some of their products was replaced with dried fruit. For the more affluent classes, the fact that servants were finding the wages at Gretna and in other factories more attractive, meant that people of all classes were having to take more account of the details of feeding their families and keeping their houses clean. The range of products during the later years of the war increased with Keatings powder (good for destroying household insects and to send to the front to deal with lice), Vim and Jeyes Fluid all being promoted.

May 18 was the date of the first Royal visit to Carlisle for 300 years. King George V and Queen Mary travelled around the north of England visiting factories and shipyards and included a visit to Gretna and Carlisle on the same day. The royal couple spent just over an hour in

King George V inspecting the guard of honour at Edenside. Ashley Kendall

The King taking the salute at Edenside. Ashley Kendall

Council workmen outside the Town Hall for the King's visit. Ashley Kendall

The King and Queen greeted by the Mayor and other dignitaries. Ashley Kendall

the city, where the visit focused on schoolchildren and munitions workers. They began by inspecting the Volunteers at the Edenside cricket ground. They drove across the Eden Bridge through crowds of school children, girls on one side the boys on the other, and along roads lined by police, the public and wounded soldiers with VAD volunteers, to get to the Market Square.

At the Town Hall they were greeted by the Mayor and other dignitaries and drove through more crowds along roads lined by Canadian lumbermen and soldiers from the Castle to the Drill Hall to see the munitions works. Theodore Carr escorted the King and Queen around the plant, which he had been largely responsible for setting up, accompanied by another city figure, James Morton of Morton Sundour. The King was introduced to the Reverend Tom Hodgson, aged fifty-six, the vicar of Kirkbampton, who worked a lathe between midday and midnight. This meant he had to cycle 14 miles from Kirkbampton and back each day and he still managed to carry out his parish duties each morning and on Sunday. The King also met 35-year-old Mrs Mary Dodds, a trainee whose husband, a sergeant in the Lonsdales, had died on the Somme.

Cover of the booklet published to commemorate the Royal visit to the shell factory. Denis Perriam

The Royal party toured the factory in what had been the Drill Hall. Denis Perriam

After viewing the Gretna Tavern. Flying the Royal Standard over the Tavern was criticised by the temperance movement. Ashley Kendall

The crowds along English Street. Ashley Kendall

The party moved on and as they entered the Gretna Tavern, where the Royal Standard was unfurled from the flagpole on the roof, the visitors were greeted by Frederick Chance. Among the guests invited were the landlords of the Control Board's public houses in the city and employees of their breweries. After inspecting the rooms, kitchens and bar they moved back to their cars and travelled across the city to Victoria Viaduct and the station where their train was waiting.

Saturday 19 May, saw the first match in the city between Workington and Carlisle Women's munitions workers football teams. Workington won and while individual skills were praised, teamwork appeared to be lacking. Teams were formed at several of the plants around Gretna and at the East Cumberland factory in the Drill Hall and Pratchitts in Carlisle. Other teams from Cockermouth, Whitehaven, Derwent Mills, Maryport and Barrow continued to play throughout the war, mostly for charity. Novelty matches were played against men's teams from the Welsh Fusiliers, who played with hands tied behind their backs, and Canadian Lumberjacks, when Carlisle Ladies won by three goals to two.

The voluntary scheme of individual food rationing was set alongside the rations for sugar, based on the population numbers.

Pratchitts' munitonettes 1917. Patrick Brennan

Carlisle Women's football team 1917-1918. Patrick Brennan

Carlisle was having difficulty convincing the Ministry of Food that the numbers had increased significantly from the 46,000 estimated from the 1911 census. The food pledge returns from one part of the city showed that there were six people living in each household, compared with an average of four for the whole city in the estimates for 1914. Many more people came to Carlisle for shopping, possibly as many as 10,000 arrived from the surrounding area, putting further pressure on the supplies of controlled goods.

The pressure on the army was shown when in late May an advert appeared in the *Journal* asking women to volunteer as clerks in the Women's Army Auxiliary Corps in France thereby releasing men for the front. The advert was careful to point out that those working in government departments and controlled industries could only apply with the written agreement of their current employer and no woman with a husband serving abroad could apply.

Children's health continued to be a cause of concern to Dr Beard, the Medical Officer. Although the loss of one doctor to the army had resulted in fewer visits, nurses had continued to inspect children and in surprise visits to schools had had to exclude 987 children who had vermin of one type or another. There were more cases of scabies, caused by a highly contagious mite which buried itself in the skin. The infestation began in 1914 brought by soldiers home on leave but it was now being passed from child to child. The 148 children who had ringworm missed nearly one term of schooling as they were excluded to prevent the infection from spreading and the treatment was slow but doctors wondered if the newly introduced use of X-ray therapy might speed up recovery. Cases of tuberculosis were reported with twenty-eight of the ninety-four children requiring treatment in the sanatorium. Parents of children with tooth decay were often unwilling to allow them to attend the clinics but some later changed their minds and most of the 581 were eventually treated; only six were found to have no decay.

The Whitsun holiday allowed some of the local workers to take a break. Over 1,500 tickets were sold for train travel to Silloth and 750 to Wetheral. Town dwellers who had cheerfully taken on an allotment soon learned that growing food was not simply a case of planting a crop and then sitting back to watch it grow. Weeding, thinning and the myriad other tasks were taking time and many men realised that between work and the allotment they had little time for other forms of leisure.

The Saturday of Whitsun was the traditional time for farm workers and farmers to attend the Hirings, when contracts for the period to Martinmas in November would be agreed. The choice of men was restricted to those above military age and boys. Men were asking £40 but the farmers held out against this and most agreements were made at prices from £30 to £36. Generally the rates being paid, which came with board and lodgings, were now about double those being paid before the war.

Education after the war was the theme of a conference in the Town Hall on 9 June attended by local MPs. Schooling, it was said, had been to prepare children ready to be cheap labour, it now had to prepare children as citizens. It was agreed that involvement in education until the age of eighteen, as enjoyed by the upper classes, should be open to all, but the problem was what curriculum could be offered? The delegates were told that Mr Fisher was looking for local authorities to be experimental in their planning, they would not be punished if they made mistakes. Progressive authorities would be encouraged and those unwilling to change would be 'pushed on'. The meeting passed a resolution to be taken by the MPs to the Minister:

> *'This meeting declares that a free educational highway from the nursery schools to the university is the only educational system which can satisfy the needs of a democratic community. As an immediate step towards this end we require the next Education Act to provide for (1) the establishment of nursery schools for children between the ages of 2 and 6; (2) the abolition of all absences except for sickness for all children between the ages of 6 and 14 with the proviso that it be raised to 15 within 5 years; (3) compulsory part-time education between the ages of 14 and 18, twenty-five hours in the workshop and twenty hours in the school room to be the normal working week for adolescents; (4) free secondary education; (5) free university education for those reaching the required standard with maintenance grants where necessary.'*

They proposed no specialisation before the age of sixteen and no class should have more than forty pupils.

A public ceremony to award gallantry medals was held at the Castle. In the two cases where the men had been killed the medals were presented to members of their family. The parents of Captain Thomas Jackson from Greystoke received the Military Cross won by their son and the brother of Private John Wedgwood accepted his Military Medal. The other four men were presented with their medals, each one receiving a loud cheer from the crowd.

By the middle of June it was evident that the military comb-out of men to go into the forces and the wider range of opportunities for women to earn good money were having an impact. Bucks, the shirt makers, advertised for girl machinists to learn shirt making and other companies specifically asked for girls to apply to learn shop duties, pack biscuits and undertake other duties. The military also announced that they would not be recalling agricultural workers before tribunals. Men who had received exemption would not be required to attend for medical re-examination or argue their case before the tribunal. Farmers greeted this with relief emphasising that it was about time. Many of them had spent valuable time presenting their cases before tribunals which agreed with them and exempted the employees only to have the military appeal two or three times, each taking time from farming.

The 'debate' between the Reverend Stuart Wilson and the Control Board continued through the letter columns of the *Journal*. The board declared that its policies of reducing the number of public houses and restricting the sale of spirits were the reasons behind the reduction. Mr Wilson argued that when he visited Carlisle at the beginning of 1917 he saw instances of drunkenness, including inebriated women, which he had not witnessed elsewhere and contended that the state scheme was responsible. One defender of the board was the Methodist minister the Reverend Bramwell Evans who, in a long letter in July, set out counter-arguments and corrections to every point in Mr Wilson's paper.

The complexity of the plethora of food orders issued during 1917 was exemplified by the trial of three confectioners on 22 June. Little and Johnson, a firm selling cakes in English Street, Mary Thornthwaite, a trader in Lowther Street and Mary Higgins of Castle Street were all summonsed for selling raspberry buns and a sandwich biscuit in contravention of the food order. The case brought some laughter into the court as the magistrates and solicitors tried to determine exactly what was intended by the order. The case hung on the regulation forbidding the addition of anything to the dough of a cake, or adding anything after the cake was completed, so the coconut-dressed cake was declared by inspectors to be illegal.

The sugar shortage was the reason behind the order and it was felt that to add fruit or jam to a mixture would exceed the permitted amount of sugar. The Chief Constable said that they had been instructed by the food inspector to bring charges as a warning to others. The magistrates imposed fines of 5s on each of the shopkeepers and warned them to avoid making raspberry buns. How far this clarified the meaning of the order is difficult to ascertain, but the confusion was evident.

The Chief Constable himself was the centre of a case on 25 June which showed the lengths that some people would go to attack those thought to have German sympathies. A retired postman, Robert Neale of Charlotte Street had been making assertions about the police in Carlisle but had more recently focused his attacks on the Chief Constable whom he evidently believed to be of German origin. Mr Neale, in 1914, had 'arrested' two schoolboys with cameras at the Citadel Station and taken them to the police station. He clearly believed that they had done something wrong but was told by the sergeant that there was no case and he was in the wrong for forcing the boys to go with him. Since then he had frequently called out at policemen in the city and had been heard to shout 'look at the German Chief Constable. Here comes the German High Commissioner!' He also made abusive comments about the sergeant in charge of training recruits. In addition to calling out comments in the street and in public houses he also shouted 'there's the German talking to the County Chief Constable!' when the Chief Constable arrived with the County Chief Constable for the Mayor's service. On 18 June he came upon the Chief Constable on the Viaduct and called him a 'dirty dog'. Mr de Schmid warned him but he persisted, was arrested and put up in court on 22 June when the case was adjourned to allow the defence solicitor time to talk with his client.

The prosecution solicitor, Mr George Lightfoot, set out Mr de Schmid's family history. He was born of British parents; his father was a naturalised Italian, who had served in the Militia for twelve years and then for a further thirty-two years a superintendent of police. Charles Dix, the defence solicitor explained that his client now acknowledged he was in error about the Chief Constable and unreservedly apologised. He had an exemplary background having retired from the Post Office in London and moved to Carlisle where he was a caretaker of one of the local chapels. He had been helpful to the police in moving on vagrants who slept near the building and had set up a club for them. He accepted that the only reason for his attacks on the Chief Constable was his name and if Germany had not been the enemy it would not have been something he worried about. He had, after talking to his solicitor, written a letter of apology to Mr de Schmid.

The magistrates warned Mr Neale that they took a very serious view of his offence but Mr de Schmid had accepted the apology and the magistrates bound over Mr Neale to be of good behaviour for twelve months. He had to find two sureties of £50 and put up one for himself for £100. If he offended again he would be imprisoned for six months.

Health, this time of infants, was the focus of 'Baby Week' a national initiative attempting to reduce the number of infants, 100,000, who died before their first birthday. The importance of Health Visitors to give advice and the centres already established in the city were popular and doing good work. The underlying problem of poor housing was more difficult to overcome and as Dr Beard commented that until men as well as women realised the importance of the matter things would not improve rapidly.

In contrast to 1916 when holidays were cancelled the traditional works closure was planned for the first week in July 1917. Silloth once again proved a popular draw, trains to the coast were packed and people unable to get a seat had to wait for services later in the day. A baseball match played between teams of Canadian forestry workers raised £30 for the Citizens' League PoW Fund.

Breaches of the food regulations resulted in more traders appearing before the magistrates in early July. The Carlisle Cafe on English Street and the manager of the Red Lion were accused of failing to keep the register showing the number of meals provided and the quantity of meat, bread and sugar used. The Carlisle Bread and Flour Company, Victoria Viaduct, was accused of selling a loaf 1oz over the full pound permitted by the order. The magistrates appreciated the difficulties of the bakers and dismissed the case, but warned the company to take care.

Like others separated from friends and family Gretna workers wanted to keep in touch. John Hughes

As the season progressed new potatoes appeared on the market and the price began to fall. Wholesale merchants discovered that while farmers were flooding the market the demand from traders and shopkeepers had declined, partly because more people were growing their own produce.

The third anniversary of the outbreak of the war led the editor of the *Journal* to run a report on the changes in the price of foodstuffs during the three years. The article pointed out, rightly or wrongly, that Carlisle had suffered from increasing prices before other parts of the country because of the influx of workers at Gretna.

Put simply most items in the housewife's shopping basket, with a few exceptions, had doubled in price. Potatoes cost 10d for 14lbs in 1914 and, even with government controls, this went up to 1s 8d; flour increased from 1s 8d to 3s 6d for a stone; oatmeal nearly tripled in price from 2s to 5s 9d. If meat and fish were unaffordable the poor depended on potatoes and bread, both items affected by U-boats and the poor harvests of 1916. One pound of tea costing 1s 4d in 1914 would set you back 2s 4d in 1917, the cost of the same amount of coffee increased from 1s to 2s and cocoa from 1s 2d to 2s. Bananas which had been unavailable in 1915 and 1916 would in 1917 cost 2s 6d for a dozen, compared to 9d in 1914. Sugar, a real staple, went from 2d a pound to 5¾d. This increase masked the fluctuation which had taken place in its price. On the outbreak of war the price jumped immediately to 7d and the government limited supplies to major town and cities based on the population censes of 1911.

In Carlisle the influx of population meant that there were always queues and families went without sugar for weeks. In the middle of 1917 the government agreed to increase Carlisle's allocation which went some way towards alleviating the situation.

The anniversary of the declaration of war was marked by a meeting outside the Town Hall. The band of the Border Regiment played to entertain the growing crowd which was gathering to listen to the Mayor and cheer as James Fell, a former railway worker who joined the Borders, receive his DCM and MM. By the time the Mayor took up his place on the top of the steps about 5,000 people were assembled.

The commemoration events continued on Sunday when there was a service in the Cathedral. The Dean spoke against 'peace without indemnities or reprisals' which the German people were promoting. He said that Germany must be punished and in part that could be achieved by returning land stolen from France fifty years earlier[1]. The Bishop of Carlisle preached at the evening service making similar points about punishing the wrongdoing of Germany without penalising individual Germans.

In late August the Food Controller went one step closer to organising a system of rationing for sugar. Traders were to be registered and allowed supplies based on the number of their customers. Householders would have to complete a form for their nominated supplier which showed the number of people in the house.

The publication of the Education Bill by Herbert Fisher was welcomed by the Carlisle press as it included many of the ideas put forward at the conference in the city in previous months. The Bill made

1 Reference to Alsace Lorraine taken by Germany during the Franco-Prussian War 1870

provision for nursery education, imposed compulsory education to the age of fourteen and part-time education to the age of eighteen. Local authorities were to draw up plans for their districts and private schools had to be as efficient as those supported by the state. Later in the month the Bishop of Carlisle took issue with some of the proposals. While he welcomed the suggestion that pupils should have better schooling he did not believe that all children would benefit from continuing part-time education to the age of eighteen. The curriculum had to be wide enough to accommodate children of all types and ensure that not everything was dependent on books. His main complaint was that insufficient attention was given to religious education and he feared that the Bill might suffer if it failed to give proper attention to this important aspect of life.

The end of summer was traditionally the time of year when people harvested or bought fruit to preserve. The sugar regulation allowed householders to purchase sugar to preserve fruit they had grown, but not that which they had obtained from elsewhere. Six defendants were accused of buying sugar to preserve fruit that they had not grown themselves. Three defendants admitted that they had technically offended, but it was through a misunderstanding. One, Mary Kennedy of the Graham's Temperance Hotel, explained that the fruit she was using she had grown in her garden at Lochmaben. She had written a letter of explanation to the Food Controller. Another, Samuel Maskell, pleaded guilty through his solicitor but explained that the fruit had been grown by his father and traditionally they had always preserved it for him, returning half of the jam in 'payment' for the fruit. Mrs Castiglione, it was alleged, submitted a form which had been altered to include the words 'or bought' alongside the 'fruit grown by us'. Mr Castiglione explained that the order was only brought in on 12 June and he contacted the Food Office in London to ask advice before his wife placed the order in May. The Chief Constable said Mrs Castiglione had indicated that the fruit was coming from a garden they owned in Edinburgh. Mr Castiglione denied that this had been said and added that he did not know who had crossed out the 'grown by us' on the form. The magistrates said that they took a serious view of these cases as many people in the city were having great difficulty in obtaining any sugar; they fined Mrs Castiglione £5 and the other defendants £2.

Mr Castiglione, found himself back in court soon after because, his solicitor claimed, he was unaware of the petrol control regulations forbidding travel to race meetings. A policeman had seen Mr Castiglione's car, with men he knew to be bookmakers in it. When questioned, Mr Castiglione said that he had been to a whippet race. His solicitor questioned whether this was a 'race meeting' as defined by the order which specifically mentioned horse racing but he did not use that as a defence. The court ordered the payment of costs of 8s 4d and a bookmaker was ordered to pay 8s costs.

Authorities were offered public money if they prepared plans to provide housing, based on an assessment of need. The Health Committee drew up a process to develop criteria and identified areas of council owned land where up to 600 houses, with space for gardens would be built. These areas covered Denton Street, Boustead's Grassing, Dalston Road, Blackwell Road, Wigton Road and Newtown Road. When the matter came before the City Council in September the Mayor proposed a separate committee be set up to deal with the development of housing. Political differences appeared with members taking party lines to argue for and against the Mayor's proposal. The Mayor explained that his reason for suggesting a separate committee was that the Health Committee had enough to do without taking on this new responsibility.

The system of food control was strengthened when local committees were established. The maximum number of members was limited to twelve and had to include a Labour representative and a woman to avoid traders dominating. It was proposed that specialist sub-committees to advise the main committee would be the way forward. Leaving two places on the committee was a good move politically as it allowed the Mayor to suggest that members might offer additional names. Having complained about the huge price increases and shortages of important items, food control was not popular since it would probably mean further price increases. The maximum price for oatmeal was fixed at a level higher than that being paid locally on the open market. Local committees could, with the agreement of the controller, make a local variation to bring the price below the maximum allowed. Carlisle's position with its large rural hinterland and good rail connections had always ensured a good supply of foodstuffs at reasonable prices and the committee was going to be under pressure to meet local expectations.

The first food order to bring comfort to Carlisle was that which controlled the price of bread. Introduced on 13 September it reduced the price of flour by 10d a stone and in consequence the price of bread was reduced by about 1d per pound. There was concern that ways used to reduce the use of flour in bread, including that addition of potato, was resulting in an increase of skin and digestive complaints.

Although originally disappointed at the impact of the control of meat the drop of another 1d per pound in mid-September encouraged people to believe that control may actually help.

With the coming of autumn and winter, clubs were established or re-opened to keep young people off the streets. One of the first clubs to reopen for the winter was the King's Hall Girls' club. Nearly 300 members arrived for the reopening when Mrs Chance and Miss Creighton with the Mayoress introduced the new club leader, Miss Harris, who had experience of club work in other parts of the country. Singing, dressmaking, fancy needlework and drill classes were planned to start in October. Traditional activities such as uniformed organisations were well supported and in mid-September Lady Baden Powell visited the city to inspect thirteen Girl Guide companies. Mr Liddell, the High Sheriff; the Dean of the Cathedral; the Mayor and Mayoress; Lady Carlisle; Colonel Mayhew, CO at the Castle, and other dignitaries were in attendance. The Border Regiment band played for the occasion and after being inspected the 500 guides demonstrated their badge skills.

Harvesting began with support from released soldiers and schoolboys from Repton and other public schools who again came to camp in the district. When preparing the land for replanting the horse drawn plough faced competition from motor tractors, one being demonstrated at Harraby which could cover the ground much more quickly than a horse by ploughing three furrows at once. Soldiers were trained to use the machines and local engineers supported by the local war agriculture committees stocked machines which farmers were able to hire. Later pictures show a farmer's daughter ploughing.

Much relief was felt when it was announced that workers would no longer need leaving certificates to change jobs. Many employers, it was believed by the unions, had claimed to the munitions tribunals that the work being done by the applicant was of military importance, even if that was not the case. A number of men had been moved to Carlisle as part of the national service scheme and were finding it increasingly difficult to keep their families and pay for lodging in Carlisle. They welcomed the opportunity to give a week's notice and return home.

Like the troops, women from Gretna sent photos home, the Anderson sisters. John Hughes

The improvement of housing, left in the hands of the Health Committee was the subject of a census, report and discussion during September and October. The census of the whole city revealed that the population stood at 56,437 (46,420 at the 1911 census) which included 6,794 lodgers. They lived in 11,892 dwellings, some being self contained (8,644), tenements (1,566) and back-to-back houses (1,682); 436 houses had no separate bedroom, 2,051 had only one bedroom. The back-to-back and tenement dwellings were closely packed and had little light and air circulating round them, sanitation and drainage was also poor. A sub-committee had worked up the details of one district to show how new houses with space and gardens would be built. Research suggests that Carlisle was unusual in carrying out a full census, other local authorities estimated numbers and the type of houses based on the 1911 census and other surveys.

The report was the main item for discussion by the City Council at the meeting on 9 October. After being criticised by the council at the previous meeting the Health Committee proposed that 2,100 houses be built, partly to house the 508 married people in lodgings and to replace the unhealthy back-to-back houses. The council welcomed the report but questioned whether to deal with the problem 'piecemeal' was the best way forward. The Mayor, probably having seen the developments at Gretna, proposed that they look to engage the services of a planner knowledgeable about 'new town' developments. Other members wanted to be able to encourage local architects, who had had little work during the war, to benefit from the schemes. Eventually the council resolved to present the scheme to the Local Government Board by the deadline but to ask for a meeting. Pressure on the electricity supply had already led the council to request permission from the Munitions Board to extend the plant. They were now going to request permission again, as if it was turned down again it would not be the council's responsibility if the supply failed to meet the needs of the city.

At the third annual meeting of the Citizens' League the routine work of the League was now around the support of PoWs in Germany and Turkey, running the rest room and working with government departments. The number of PoWs being supported had risen from 163 on 1 December 1916 to nearly 450, many of them from the Lonsdales. It was suggested that individuals or churches and groups of workers might 'adopt' a prisoner and collect funds on his behalf. The system seemed to be working well for the men being held in Germany as the League and families got letters confirming that the parcels were getting through.

The 300 citizens helping to run the Rest Room in Court Square had served nearly 375,000 meals during the year and about 15,000 men had spent the night; the demand for baths had been so high that the hot water supply was increased. One area of work which had been less successful than in 1916 was the supply of eggs. In 1916 about 30,000 eggs had been collected and distributed but in 1917 the number had fallen to 11,000 reflecting the general shortage.

Having failed first time round, the relaunched national service scheme was attempting to attract support. The director spoke about the need for more people to join the workforce and particularly mentioned that most of the women involved so far were from the working or upper classes; few wives of middle class families had joined the scheme.

Sallie Brown and Gertie Tuffen. Gertie was a kitchen maid born in Carlisle who was working in Brampton aged 20 in 1911. Ashley Kendall

Contact was important for those away as well as those left behind in Carlisle.
John Hughes

The fox hunting season began earlier than normal to allow the hunts to get to grips with the reportedly increased number of animals in country districts. The Border Coursing meeting, which was traditionally held on land now covered by the munitions works, appeared to be doomed but on 17 and 18 October it was resurrected on new land at Cubby Hill.

An acknowledgement by the temperance parties of the work by the Control Board appeared in the *Journal* of 12 October when John Kendal, secretary of the City Borders Sons of Temperance, wrote:

> *'We thank the Control Board for what it has accomplished in our city and hope it will resist the attempt being made to reopen public houses on Sundays.'*

In the same edition there was a report that the opening of the Citadel Tavern in English Street, which replaced the Three Crowns and

The interior of the Wellington Hotel which was remodelled as part of the Citadel Tavern. John Hughes

Wellington Hotels, marked the end of the first stage of the refurbishment of public houses in the city.

Restaurateurs began to feel the pressure of competition from the state-owned restaurants. Their complaint was that the Control Board used the alcohol regulations to require public houses to provide food. One correspondent in the letters page argued that the cost of meals in restaurants was regulated by the government at well below the amount necessary to cover the cost of refurbishing the buildings. He estimated the cost of the Citadel Tavern to be about £20,000 but this had been provided by the board. The privately owned places were unable to provide the quality of fittings and furnishings seen in the taverns. The need for 'ordinary' caterers to compete with the regulated prices, pay for their premises and staff when the highly paid officials were civil servants and the buildings were subsidised was very unfair and he appealed to other tradesmen to consider how they would feel if the government opened subsidised jewellers and drapers. Richard Denman MP raised the question in parliament but was told that the Treasury could not see how the small trader was put at a disadvantage.

Price controls for butter and milk were introduced from mid-October. The price of butter, which in 1914 was 1s per pound was fixed at 2s 2d per pound; the market price in the previous week had been 2s 4d. The milk traders had been talking about increasing the price to 7d for two pints but the price was fixed by the Food Committee at 6d.

A high-powered working group had been set up in 1916 and led by Canon Rawnsley and Miss Creighton, and was now ready to suggest ideas for providing worthwhile activities for the young people of the city. The Dean, Mr Campbell, the Chief Constable, Mr Chance, Mrs Graham and Miss Henderson were among those who gathered together to discuss the proposals. Canon Rawsley said:

> *'This meeting is important to deal with the welfare of the young people of Carlisle not only for the good of the city but for the country and Empire. It is good that the Home Office has woken up to the problem and Carlisle might well be proud of having anticipated the desire of the Home Office in having set going machinery which without any important changes will meet the Home Office scheme.'*

The scheme Carlisle was ahead of asked each local authority to establish a committee representing all organisations concerned with the welfare of boys and girls between the ages of twelve and nineteen. A Juvenile Welfare Association for Carlisle and district was established which had representatives of the clubs and uniformed organisations already operating in the district. In addition they invited representation from the Education Committee, the Juvenile Advisory Committee and the National Union of Teachers. This group was to support and encourage existing groups and look for alternative activities to widen engagement.

The Carlisle committee had asked clubs and associations to report on their activities. The Central Boys' Club opened in January 1917, meeting in the Boys' Brigade Institute. Robert Chance and George Saul were amongst the committee. The club had over 500 members of whom about 350, mainly errand boys and paper boys mostly from poorer homes, attended regularly. It provided a gym, reading room and games room and a canteen provided refreshments. There was a service on most Sunday evenings, led by Mr Chance and the boys could use the public baths at a reduced charge. A children's club ran for five weeks and during that time 1,500 children attended to participate in needlework, raffia work, picture framing and games. The experience gained from the running of this centre encouraged the committee to look for other places to open similar centres. A report on child employment had investigated the position in other towns and cities and suggested amendments to the local by-laws to raise the age of those permitted to trade in the streets from twelve to fourteen. They also proposed to the Home Office that no school age child should be allowed in a cinema after 9pm.

One of the new activities for young people was the offer of talks and visits arranged by the Board for Juvenile Employment. This organisation used to simply place school leavers into vacancies in local factories. They decided to give information about what was involved in some of the jobs and the background to the industries. Talks on topics such as 'The Cotton Plant' were arranged for older pupils. Only 140 of the 750 who applied to hear the lecture by Dr Overton were able to be fitted into Tullie House but the success of this venture encouraged the board to plan other events including factory visits.

Lord Rhondda the Food Controller, warned at the beginning of October that unless people cut down on the amount they were eating the government would have to introduce compulsory rationing. Unlike 1916 there had been a good crop of potatoes and it was anticipated that there would not be a shortage and he encouraged families to eat more potatoes and vegetables to replace foods based on grain; in contrast to 1916 in some adverts housewives were told how to make bread using potatoes to reduce the amount of flour.

Fusehill Hospital opened on 15 October. It had auxiliary units across the county catering separately for officers and other ranks: Barrow-in-Furness Military Hospital had 115 beds for other ranks; there were thirteen beds for other ranks at Carlisle Military Hospital; Hazlebank Auxiliary Hospital, Gosforth and Broadleys at Windermere had twelve and twenty beds respectively for officers. The recently created hospital in Newtown School, Carlisle provided eighty beds for other ranks. The other hospitals remained under the control of Fazakerley: Chadwick VAD Hospital, with forty-five beds for other ranks, and its annexe, Castleton Auxiliary Hospital; Cumberland Infirmary, had thirty beds, all for other ranks, and Murrell Hill Hospital, Carlisle, forty beds.

Merchants from other cities threatened farmers' wives who came to Carlisle market because they were holding back supplies to cater for their regular customers. The traders were from parts of the country where locally produced butter was expensive because imports from Denmark and Holland had ceased. Prices in these areas were well above those in Carlisle so it was profitable to purchase butter here and transport it to where they could command a higher price.

On 5 November Lord Leverhulme of Port Sunlight visited the city to lecture the Chamber of Commerce about 'After the war problems'. He encouraged the businessmen of the city to look to the period after the war, not fall into the old British trap of always doing things the same way, but also look at important social issues like the shortage of housing.

Matches were in short supply, some blamed the Control Board, others the warehouses which were slow in meeting orders and others the transport system. Whatever the cause those who had matches went to some lengths to keep them safe which sometimes led to munitions workers ending up in court. On 3 November six workers were taken to court, most had put pipes, tobacco matches or cigarettes into the lockers as required by law but were found with extra matches in handkerchiefs or inside pockets having forgotten they were there. Jane Carr, the first woman to be found with matches at one factory, was put before the magistrates. Her solicitor pleaded for leniency as she had eleven children to look after and cycled into Carlisle from Rockcliffe to do her work. After due consideration the magistrates fined the men £10 and Jane Carr £1.

The war news through most of 1917 was predominantly of Allied advances and German and Turkish retreats. No week passed without ten or twenty Carlisle men being included in the lists of killed, wounded and missing and the number of widows in the city, or families of men who returned maimed continued to rise. Those appealing against being called up were less likely to be successful.

The Belgian Refugee Committee held its third annual meeting on 23 November. Miss Creighton reported that there were still seventy Belgian refugees in the city, mostly women and children though there were twelve men, a number of whom were likely to be called up in the near future.

Fish was in very short supply because of recent storms and prices rose to four or five times higher than in 1914, cod having risen from 6d to 2s 3d a pound. The market price of cattle, both for milk and for meat, moved through previous record amounts on a weekly basis during December. The demand for butter and milk resulted in farmers buying more dairy cattle, the lack of imported meat attracted farmers to keeping more beef stock for fattening.

Anti-German feeling continued; some shopkeepers in various parts of the country, including Carlisle, changed the names over their premises. In a change announced in the *London Gazette* of 4 December and reported in the *Journal* of 7 December, the Chief Constable who in June had been accused of German ancestry resulting in the trial of his accuser, adopted his grandmother's family name of Spence.

The first full meeting of the Carlisle Juvenile Welfare Association was held on 12 December. Responding to concerns about the behaviour of young people, as young as six or seven in some cases, Canon Rawnsley and others had met to consider what the city might do to resolve the situation. Like the meeting in October many of those attending were well respected and concerned about life in the city. Major Robert Chance, Henry Campbell, Canon Rawnsley, Mrs Rashdall, wife of the new Dean, Miss Creighton, Miss Henderson,

Joseph Duckworth, the schools' superintendent, were among the members of the committee set up to further the work.

Food shortage and queues were leading to frustration in all towns and cities. A Newcastle councillor suggested that if men had to queue instead of their wives a solution would be found quickly. Birmingham council developed local rationing and issued to every holder of a sugar card an additional card for use in shops. The Birmingham Food Control Committee would announce what quantities of each of tea, butter, margarine and flour and other items would be allowed each week depending on the amount of each held in the warehouses.

International changes were reported. The Russian Revolution which put Kerensky in charge and removed the Czar from the throne had implications for Britain as the two Royal families were related. It was suggested that Czar Nicholas with the Czarina and their children should be allowed to come to Britain and safety. The politicians feared that if the Romanoffs arrived in Britain local Bolsheviks would rise to revolution here. America had entered the war in 1917 but although the press locally and nationally extolled the virtues of the trained army and America's industrial might, it took time for American troops to arrive, their generals were unwilling to serve under British or French command and they brought very few large guns or other equipment with them.

During 1917 many aspects of the war affected the civilian population for the first time. Not all were managed well by the government. Britain depended on food imports from the Empire and when these were interrupted it took time to grow replacements, even if it was possible. Items were in short supply at different times so early in the year there was a mammoth potato shortage, but by the end of the year potato was being used to replace flour in bread to preserve stocks of wheat. The

Plus ça change. A card sent to Harry Mills before his wedding. John Hughes

potato riots of early 1917 were replaced by the butter and sugar queues and disturbances of the autumn. Allotment holders produced quantities of potatoes and other vegetables to supplement the commercial supplies.

Voluntary rationing had partly worked but the price of basic commodities increased hugely. One pound of butter, costing 1s in 1914, had doubled to 2s by April 1917 and with price control was held at 2s 4d, but supplies were low. Meat had increased in price, in December beef cost the housewife up to 1s 8d a pound and mutton was the same price, in April both could be bought for 1s 2d. Fish which in April was a good, but not always popular, replacement for meat cost 1s 2d for a pound of cod, but by December supplies of all types of fish were limited and the prices, when available, were high. Attempts at controlling price and regulating the supplies in the shops and market met with varying degrees of success. Another local control committee had been established to set prices and monitor stocks but the attempt with sugar cards showed the difficulty of piecemeal rationing and indicated the way forward was the use of individual cards for each person which, when introduced in Birmingham, had been shown to be more easily administered.

One product which remained available was bacon. Cavaghan & Gray at Harraby had expanded their output of bacon and ham. The bulk of the increase was to meet an army order but by advertising for carcasses and working with producers they maintained a local supply to the north of England and southern Scotland which meant that there was no shortage. Not content with using established producers the company had spoken to the government about raising pigs in Carlisle and explored connections with a company in East Africa which was interested in raising pigs and could provide regular supplies for bacon production.

Carlisle was less directly affected by the war than many places; there were no Zeppelins or bombers flying over the city although the lighting restrictions were as strictly imposed as those places more likely to be attacked. The building of HM Factory, Gretna a short distance away brought a huge increase in population, judged to be about 10,000, but during the 1917 the nature of that population changed. The navvies and labourers who had invaded the city in 1916 and stayed until early 1917 were replaced by girls and women aged 16-30. Some men, mainly those medically unfit for the army, also arrived to work at the munitions factory and all of them wanted somewhere to live. Although many found accommodation in the houses and hostels built at Gretna and Longtown many more had to look to Carlisle. The result was huge pressure on the available housing stock and the refusal of the Munitions Board to recognise the problem prevented the city from building houses to relieve the situation.

The high wages paid at Gretna attracted many men and women from the more manual and service jobs they would have undertaken in the city. They also had comparatively huge spending power resulting in high prices and making the position of ordinary workers worse. Others in the city, particularly the shopkeepers, benefitted from the influx of women with money to spend and adverts in the local papers for current fashions and changing styles did not diminish. The adverts aimed at women workers increased as did those showing time-saving products to help housewives who had lost their maid and had to do more for themselves, as well as the more prosperous working mother who now had less time to do the housework.

Many of the male workers indulged in drinking and the Control Board, set up to manage the public houses in the city, was a lasting legacy of the war remaining in business until 1971. The main indicator of success for the board was the reduction in the amount of drunkenness in the city. The sale of spirits at only certain times and the closing of public houses on Sundays and around some holidays controlled the outlets and this, coupled with limited supplies of beer which even when it was in stock was weaker, meant that cases of drunkenness continued to fall. The Chief Constable's annual report to the licensing sessions showed a continued reduction in the number of cases of drunkenness during 1917. Of the 329 cases 207 were workers from Gretna leaving 113 as residents of the city, or people travelling through, a figure well below those reached in the pre-war years.

Military and munitions tribunals continued to meet to ensure that men who should go were joining the army and those that were needed for other essential war work were retained. Those men and women in munitions and allied factories were similarly controlled, but the iniquity of the process for the men who had been 'posted' to Carlisle and Gretna having volunteered for war service under the ill-starred national service scheme was redeemed when some were allowed to return home.

THE EBB AND FLOW OF DRUNKENNESS IN CARLISLE.

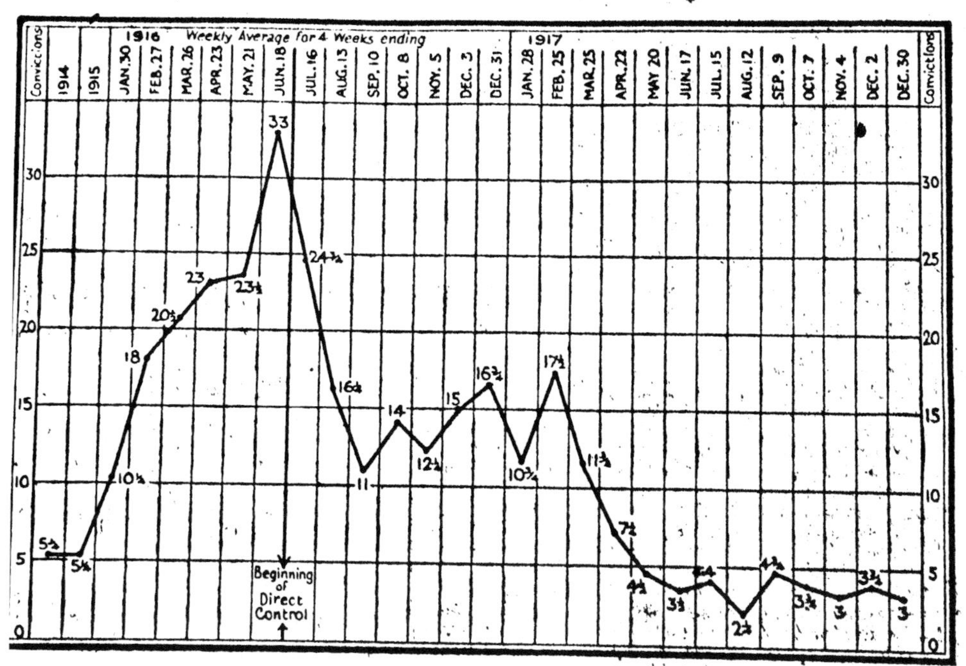

The Control Board did reduce the number of convictions. Cumbrian Newspapers Ltd

A few cases, mainly involving women, appear strange in the list of offences for which employees were brought before the magistrates. Discoveries in the personal search rooms of small pieces of what was described as cotton waste were punished quite severely. It is probable that the material was actually cordite which the workers chewed. The heady mix of ether and other chemicals gave them a high similar to that they had if exposed in the works; to recover they had to go outside for a break.

Reports on industrial activity which were printed in detail in 1914 and 1915 were less open than in previous years because security and censorship made it impossible to name companies and list activities associated with the conflict. The increase in wages to compete with Gretna, the payment of war bonuses by most employers and the increased amount of overtime meant that in many cases salaries were fifty to one hundred per cent higher than before the war. Beneficiaries of the improved income were the shopkeepers who, when they had something to sell, were surrounded by keen buyers willing to pay high prices.

Huge increases in the need to transport munitions and war supplies led to a steady reduction in the number of passenger trains. Many former express and passenger train drivers had been transferred to working freight. The handling of casualties from hospital trains had improved and the process of transferring men to hospitals was now progressing smoothly.

More importantly to local businesses, it was harder to obtain wooden packing cases. The military needed robust timber boxes for the carriage of shells and bullets and had first call on available supplies. Local companies advertised for boxes and crates. Carr's were making a reduced range of biscuits for the home market but the demand from the army and navy meant that the company was kept busy.

Hudson Scott, tin box makers, were fully engaged in making munitions but there was some demand for metal boxes. Reduced numbers of workers and shortages of metal and paper had limited output of their traditional products. The company attempted to address the shortage of workers by employing women, attracting some by providing a nursery for babies.

Morton Sundour were progressing the manufacture of dyes, a necessary adjunct to their normal tapestry and carpet making. Having been forced to experiment with dye making to overcome the shortage of dyes usually obtained from Germany the company, with government help, had extended its range of colours causing envy among many other textile dyers and spinners.

Textile firms were kept busy by the army. The Shaddon Mill worked a regular day, limited by government directions which forbade overtime. Paton's, part of the Shaddon works, was busy making curtains and other textiles for export. Ferguson's and Buck's had both suffered from the loss of staff, though Buck's had opened a plant in Londonderry which reduced pressure on supplies and workers.

Allied progress during the summer gave hope that the war would soon be ended and the thoughts of government and local politicians and others turned to 'life after the conflict'. Fisher's attempt to reform education by his Bill attracted local support, but also some opposition.

Eventually it was withdrawn but not before ideas had been shared and the need to prepare children better for adult life not just train them for a life of factory work or labouring was recognised. Even the designs for Control Board public houses were 'modern' and reflected the latest architectural ideas.

By the end of the year many of the issues which would be faced in 1918 were becoming very evident: German resurgence; the need for more troops but also more workers; the limited supplies of food. On the positive side women were more involved in work than ever before and being allowed by men to take a greater role. The munitions factory at Gretna was in full production providing huge quantities of cordite to make a wide range of munitions.

Personal life also continued. Jeanie Anderson, the Gretna munitions worker whose family lived in Carlisle and who in 1915 had given up her job as a servant on a farm at Longtown, achieved the position of chargehand, managing a team in part of the factory. One member of her group was Harry Mills, the potters' turner from Stoke whose poor

Harry Mills and Jeanie Anderson on their wedding day. John Hughes

Congratulation card for the new Mr and Mrs Mills. John Hughes

Where they lodged with the bride's family in Tilbury Road. John Hughes

eyesight kept him out of the army. Both living in Carlisle the two had met and courted on the train from Gretna back to their homes in the city. On Christmas Eve 1917 they were married by the Reverend Frederick Millard in St Aidan's Church. Jeanie's football playing sister Annie was one of the witnesses and after their marriage the happy couple lived with Jeanie's parents in Tilbury Road.

CHAPTER 7

1918: Turmoil and Triumph

Strike at the brewery – Improved conditions at Carr's – Council problems over supply of gas, electricity, housing and trams – Frustration of military tribunal members – Measles outbreak – Food controls strengthened – Carlisle buys a destroyer – Confusion of Food Control Committee – Effect of German Spring Offensive – Women tram drivers – Draconian controls on jam makers – Replacements for farm workers – OBE for Gretna women – Sunday concert in Bitts Park – Butter control outcry – 'Spanish' flu outbreak – Recycling and salvage – Rationing of coal, coke, electricity and gas – International journalists visit Carlisle – Praise for the Citizens' League – Italian band in Carlisle – Magistrates deal with ration dodgers – Recruiting women – Armistice, celebration and sorrow – End of conscription – General election.

The shortages continued, not in shells as stocks were established and the scale of fighting was diminishing so demand was falling, but in domestic foodstuffs and home essentials like fuel. In the coldest part of the year there were complaints about the quality of coal being supplied. The local supplies from Durham and Cumberland were seen as of poorer quality than the Yorkshire coal preferred by the citizens of Carlisle.

Industrial relations went awry at the State Breweries over the New Year. Before Christmas a request for a 5s a week pay rise had been submitted and rejected. The union had acknowledged the rejection but there had been no further discussion. Traditionally the workers in the brewery received a pint of beer at 12.30pm each afternoon, to avoid breaching the local regulation banning morning drinking. On New Year's Day some of the workers were carrying out essential tasks before breakfast and would have a holiday once this work was completed. Finishing before 12.30 the workers expected to receive their pint and were annoyed to have it withheld as it was too early. They immediately went on strike and refused to return the following morning. The board eventually managed to talk to the union representative and the men agreed to return if discussions about their wage demands were reinstated. This was refused and the strike continued. During the following week members of the Railwaymen's Union were told of the strike and agreed to drink no beer or ale until the strike was resolved. The workers returned to the brewery on 12 January.

Care of workers improved at Carr's. Refreshments and social breaks for office workers were unusual in 1918 when Carr's opened a room for staff to meet and chat over coffee or other drinks during the working day. Staff unable to get home at lunchtime could use the room to eat their sandwiches.

Housewives had difficulty finding supplies of margarine on 3 January and spent many hours fruitlessly searching and queuing, one shop had an estimated 500 people waiting outside. The Woolwich Co-op had introduced cards for its members who found no difficulty in using them to buy many essential items including tea, butter and margarine. At a meeting of grocers the request was made to the Food Committee to ensure an equitable distribution of butter and margarine and all grocers agreed to publish a list of prices in their window.

Shortages of meat, leading to queues in many cities, were blamed by the farmers on the price fixing that had occurred in the autumn. Rather than pass on stock for fattening many farmers had been forced to sell animals for slaughter resulting in smaller beasts being available and stocks running out. The usual positions were taken with farmers protesting that they were not being paid enough to cover costs and the urban dwellers suspecting that farmers were withholding stocks to force up prices.

The first council meeting of 1918 dealt with the housing proposals of the Health Committee and in view of the increased size of the project, building 2,100 houses and dealing with the congested areas in the centre of the city, established a special sub-committee to deal with the issue.

The Gas Committee, faced with increased costs of coal, now costing over 23s per ton, compared with 11s 3d in 1914, oil which had gone up by five times from its pre-war price of 3½d per gallon and wages which had risen by sixty to seventy per cent, proposed a price increase which would triple the pre-war cost to the consumer. The council had refused to sanction an increase to 3s 3d for 1,000cubic feet and the committee proposed an increase to 3s, compared with 1s in 1914. The equipment at the gas works was obsolete and was using the technology available in 1853, so a review was desperately needed to ensure that supplies did not break down.

Letters informing families of the death of loved ones continued to arrive. One of the respected Carlisle men who died of his wounds on 13 January 1918 was Corporal Henry Rolt, for twenty-two years a schoolmaster at Lowther Street School. He joined the army at the age of forty-three, above the minimum age in 1915 and was promoted to quartermaster sergeant a rank he relinquished to join a draft for France. He died serving in the Army Service Corps transporting ammunition in a lorry which was hit by a shell. A Freemason, secretary of the Carlisle Sports Committee and of the Cavendish Tennis Club, he was well known in the city for organising charity events. His widow and two children, aged eleven and five were living in Lowther Street.

As happened in 1917 the Appeals Tribunal Members became frustrated at the way in which the authorities were appealing or refusing to accept referrals to the medical boards. The local representative of national service said that it was a head office decision to appeal against all referrals of men in A and B categories; tribunal members protested that this was a waste of their time; they should be allowed to do their job.

The tribunal refused five of the appeals by the military for men from the Co-op. Hudson Scott, a company said by their representative to be spending seventy-five per cent of their time on government work, opposed the appeals against the exemption of three of their men, a cost clerk, box maker and order clerk. Of the ninety men of military age employed by the company no more than a dozen were fit for military

Recruiting Office staff were still hard pressed in 1918. Time was found for a group picture outside the Crown and Mitre Hotel. Denis Perriam

service, but the military representative added 'it depends what is meant by fit'. The Town Clerk observed that the tribunal was aware of local circumstances and if they did not do their duty they may as well close down some of the businesses in the city. All the military appeals were disallowed.

There were 461 cases of measles among children in December and more occurred in January; some of the victims had recovered but then succumbed to bronchitis or pneumonia. The cause was thought to be the poor weather but people were not staying at home if they were ill and those moving from place to place to try to find food were also blamed for the spread. One teacher whose school was closed was sent to another one where the disease spread.

A revised Education Bill was introduced which reduced the level of control to be taken by the Board of Education, leaving more with local authorities. The implications for the city were explained by Joseph Duckworth, the superintendent of schools. The reduction in class size meant that they would have to put new partitions in schools to divide two classes of sixty pupils into three of forty. The designation of all education after the age of twelve as secondary had implications for the subjects offered and the need to provide day training for those aged fourteen and above would need rooms and equipment for the 800 pupils who left school and would return for their eight hours of education each week until the age of eighteen. Accommodation for the industrial students could be provided at Tullie House for the first year. Commercial students would use two houses which had been identified and domestic students could use the existing cookery centres. Once the scheme was in full operation there would be 3,000 students so specialist accommodation would have to be provided. Teachers could be found and they would hope to engage some who had industrial experience to ensure that the training was relevant to work.

The Chance family were in the news when their three sons were all at home at transitional stages in their military careers. Major Edward Chance, who had been given command of a battalion of Northumberland Fusiliers, was home on leave. His youngest brother, Miles, was recovering from a serious wound received at Messines and Robert, who had been rejected three times as being unfit for military service and had commanded a battalion of the Cumberland Volunteers, had at last been accepted for home service with the Horse Guards; he was going to work at the headquarters in London.

Food queues were even longer outside the shops and in the market on 19 January when many butchers' shops posted signs saying 'no meat' or in others 'only half of normal orders available'. Butter, margarine and cheese were also in short supply and fish was unavailable. At the beginning of the war people were encouraged to keep poultry to provide both eggs and meat. Birds Custard was one item that advertised itself as enabling working mothers to feed their families economically and without cutting into shortage products.

At the beginning of February compulsory rationing of meat and fats, butter and margarine, was introduced. A more radical solution was proposed at a

Products to make expensive food items go further were increasing in number.
Cumbrian Newspapers Ltd

mass meeting in Carlisle on 3 February. The meeting in the new public hall in Chapel Street had been called by the Carlisle Trades and Labour Council and the Carlisle South End Co-operative Society. The resolution for discussion called on the government not only to introduce rationing to share the hardships across both rich and poor and to prevent hoarding, but to take over all farm land. It also proposed 'all food, whether produced in this country or imported to be bought by the government and sold at reasonable prices'. The proportion of working people on local food committees should be increased to better represent the needs of the consumer and the use of foodstuffs to produce alcoholic liquors should be banned. One speaker suggested that the control of food should be placed in the hands of working people. Differences between town and country, partly reflecting the political nature of those attending, rose again in the meeting. A workers representative member of the county military tribunal said that on one hand farmers were appealing for the release from military service of their rabbit catchers, claiming that crops were being destroyed by these pests, then they appealed for their gamekeepers who kept working men from catching rabbits for food.

A belief that the Food Committee was not doing its job was strengthened because individuals were found rejoining a queue having bought items in short supply and attempting to 'go round again' to get more. Members of families were known to be shopping in different parts of the city to get as much as they could, while workers at Gretna were said to be buying food in both Gretna and Carlisle. Farmers were also feeling badly done to as they felt that the Ministry of Agriculture was failing to defend the cause of the farmers against the demands of the Food Controller. Food shortages and long hours of work led some workers to risk court by pilfering items of small value, particularly from Carr's where the evidence could be eaten. Women were fined for stealing sugar and dried fruit. The magistrates warned that future cases would be punished even more severely.

Rationing moved a step closer when, on 6 February a conference of representatives of the various Food Control Committees met to consider the best way to introduce a full scheme for the north-west.

The Citizens' League was given the task of organising the city collection for the Businessmen's Week to sell War Savings in March. The national target was to sell £100,000,000 worth of war bonds; the

Carlisle target was £150,000, the price of a destroyer. The bonds, each costing 15s 6d would be worth £1 in five years. During the week of collection a model of a destroyer was loaned by Hawthorn Leslie of Newcastle and the Admiralty agreed to the showing of films about the launching and trials of a destroyer. A circular was to be sent to all farmers pointing out the benefits of war bonds as investments. Local cinemas and theatres entered into the spirit of the scheme by offering free entry to those purchasing bonds from their box offices.

There were a growing number of complaints about the quality of the tram service. The council referred the matter to the general purposes committee charging it to deal robustly with the matter. The electric works and the increasing demand for power had been exercising the council for some time. It was finally agreed that loans to improve the plant would be made available.

Major change to the supply of food was brought into force on 19 February when the slaughter of all stock was moved to the Carlisle abattoir and the other slaughter houses, including those owned by the railway companies, were closed. Farmers could send stock straight to slaughter after which it would be distributed to local butchers' shops for sale. The removal of a stage in the marketing process met the demands of butchers for meat to be sold by deadweight so, it was

The tramway and stone setts in Warwick Road. John Hughes

hoped, there would be little objection to the scheme, though some farmers complained it was reducing the amount they were paid. Traders brought rabbits for sale to the market, but these were commandeered by the Food Controller who graded them and paid the supplier before putting them up for sale at the fixed prices.

The position of the Infirmary in the health of the city came under criticism when its committee declined to provide space for a venereal disease clinic. The *Journal* leader disapproved of this decision, which forced the city council to provide space in a house in the city. The council had been told it was a requirement for it to provide a clinic and the refusal of the Infirmary to co-operate, largely because of money, was likened to its refusal to treat returned soldiers, which had to be solved by the War Office reallocating the twelve beds it paid for.

Businessmen's week, to collect money by the sale of war bonds drew to a close on Friday 8 March. Businesses had used their advertising space in the local papers to encourage the purchase of bonds and many had offered bonds or contributions to bonds as part of a purchase. Before the week ended the city had raised more than enough to buy its destroyer. The target of £150,000 (£6.5million today) had been passed with £28,000 to spare and it was anticipated that by the end of the campaign the total could exceed £200,000 (£8.25m). The additional amount, it was hoped, would be used 'to buy an aeroplane or two'. The ability of the Citizens' League to organise events to support the war had again been demonstrated.

Companies and individuals had made huge contributions, from Carr's biscuit works came £25,000, the company's flour mill contributed £10,000, Creightons, gave £17,000, Hudson Scott and Cowans Sheldon each gave £5,000, and the workers at the East Cumberland Shell Factory donated £1,000. Individuals like the Chance family, the Gibbings, the Thompsons and the Storeys each gave over £1,000. By the middle of the month the final figures for the counties were published which showed that Carlisle had purchased a destroyer; Maryport eleven aeroplanes; Whitehaven nineteen; Workington thirty and Kendal fourteen aeroplanes.

Early March saw the beginning of a German advance, known as Operation Michael, the Spring Offensive. The Allied forces confronted the German armies, which were reinforced by troops released from the eastern front by the Russian armistice. The German command realised that once the Americans arrived in numbers they would be overwhelmed and their last chance of achieving victory was to defeat the British and French quickly. The British troops by this stage were mainly conscripted men with little training. They bore the brunt of the attack, more established battalions were moved back to the Somme to face the Germans once their lines of supply had become stretched.

The military tribunal meeting on 8 March considered, among other cases, that of 36-year-old Harold Carr. He was described as manager of the domestic business, responsible for managing the whole of the home biscuit production, a branch of the business unknown to either Bertram or Theodore Carr. They were receiving thousands of orders for biscuits for the army and many people were finding it impossible to eat the war loaf and were transferring to biscuits. If Harold Carr was sent to the army not only would they lose his expertise immediately but once the war ended he would be out of touch with the work, thereby damaging the business. He was given exemption, as were thirty of the firm's employees, but another twelve were called up. However, the appeal tribunal held in Carlisle on 4 April reversed the decision and disallowed Harold Carr's appeal, but he was not to be called up until 1 May and was given permission to appeal to the central tribunal.

The city council meeting on 12 March discussed the poor and dirty state of the tramways and announced that they had requested an inspection of the service. The members could understand the increasing frustration of the population but some pointed out that enquiries of other cities and towns showed that tramways generally were falling into a poor state of repair as engineers and materials were both in great demand by the military.

The supply and control of food which had passed to local committees was held up by government announcements which were not supported by action. The publication of an order dealing with the use of sugar for jam making on 30 March resulted in hundreds of applications for the necessary forms; the Carlisle food committee had received thirty copies, and only got another 500 after asking for more but they were still unable to meet the demand.

The committee had one executive officer who had written to tender his resignation as he felt unable to carry out his duties. He had no real authority but received all the complaints about the various systems. Butchers protested that they had not received enough meat to fulfil all the rations they had registered; others apparently received too much. He took this up with the livestock commission which dealt with the supply of meat from the markets and was told it was the responsibility of the food committee to deal with the anomalies but it was impossible as they had already told the livestock people how much to send to each butcher so why was it his responsibility to balance the mistakes? This and the sugar for jam were the latest examples of issues he had had to deal with on his own in the last seven months and he could not continue. After discussion it was agreed that he would carry on allowing the committee to talk to the city council about the problems.

The committee also had to deal with cases where individuals were accused of hoarding, but again government advice was often non-committal. When an item was in good supply or there was a glut if housewives took steps to preserve it was this judged to be 'hoarding'? A number of committees had received unhelpful answers about the practice of pickling eggs during the spring and summer when there was plenty, and then using the pickled eggs in the months when hens did not lay so readily. An announcement in mid-April gave individuals the right to purchase eggs for preserving on condition they tell local committees how many they were using. Some families had asked advice about whether they were allowed to buy and store tinned meat in case they went away on holiday and were unable to transfer their meat coupons; again the advice was unclear.

A happy event reported in the *Journal* of 5 April was the announcement of the engagement of Canon Rawnsley to 44-year-old Eleanor Simpson of The Wray, Grasmere, his secretary.

A less happy notification was that of the wounding of 20-year-old Lieutenant Stanley Campbell, the son of Nicol Campbell, superintendent at Carlisle station. A member of the Border Regiment, Stanley Campbell had been wounded once before in June 1917 just two weeks after his arrival in France. His second wound was more serious resulting in a stay in hospital in Rouen, but he was transferred to a hospital in England. Twenty-seven other men were listed as being killed or wounded in this edition, the greatest number for many weeks. Three of the men left widows and families and among the wounded was a compositor who had worked for the *Journal*. As casualty lists begin to arrive from the chaos of the British retreat so the number of names increased.

A breakthrough in transport was arrived at when the committee set up to review the tramway service agreed to licence women drivers from 31 July. The service had lost men to the war and the timetable was very erratic, the company had been fined for allowing unlicensed drivers, although they were trained to drive, and so the committee had to at last admit that women could perhaps manage the routes. When the matter came before the city council it was resolved that they would, reluctantly, allow women drivers, largely because women had shown themselves capable of working in other fields usually reserved for men. Mr Wray, the company's engineer, assured the committee that all would be safe, and that if they could employ women as drivers the men who should have been repairing track but because of the unwillingness to employ women had been forced to take up driving, could return to their proper jobs and ensure that the track was maintained.

Food restrictions were imposed thick and fast. From 6 April all cooked, canned, preserved and potted meat had to be bought from the ration. Farmers were told to increase production of potatoes and were guaranteed £7 a ton for any of the 1917 crop that they were unable to sell previously. One market trader was fined for selling butter and eggs; Jeannie Millican had been offering buyers of eggs the opportunity to buy butter, she said she had a lot of eggs but while she could sell all her butter to regular customers she was having difficulty with the eggs. The magistrates accepted she had made a mistake but fined her £2 including costs. Supplies of food were further damaged when on 5 April a fire broke out at the Harraby works of Cavaghan and Gray, bacon and ham curers.

A full meat rationing scheme was introduced on 17 April. Over the winter and into spring householders had applied for cards which contained tickets which they could exchange for meat at the butcher with which they were registered. Even though the scheme was new and had been postponed new changes were coming, notably the introduction of extra rations for those undertaking heavy work and full rations for children aged six and above, rather than ten as was originally proposed; bacon and ham were to be added to the ration from 5 May. Beef and mutton had to be purchased from the family's registered butcher, pork and offal could be obtained from any butcher, but coupons had to be handed over, as they did if rabbit, poultry or game were purchased.

Eating meals in restaurants also cost coupons but the amount of meat received may not be the full five ounces allowed for raw meat. Having introduced the meat rationing scheme the Food Controller found himself under criticism because the time allowed for fruit growers to apply for sugar to make jams spanned the Easter period and did not allow time for forms to be issued and returned. The final straw was the requirement for the form to be signed by a JP, clergyman, member of the local control board or somebody who could be verified from a reference book or directory, presumably lawyers and accountants. In consequence these men were inundated with requests for their signature.

One thing the Food Controller did which was appreciated in the hill districts was to allow packs of hounds to keep feeding the dogs at the same level as when they were hunting. This allowed hunting on upland areas to continue longer than usual because it was regularly asserted that the number of foxes harrying sheep had increased during the war; an extended season would, it was hoped, allow more Herdwick lambs to survive.

The German advance in April had cost men, although the Allies began to push back and the Americans were arriving. Lloyd George announced on 9 April that in order to ensure a supply of troops into the winter he was requiring all men under the age of twenty-five to be released from what they were doing to join the army. One hundred thousand men were to be taken from munitions joining 30,000 miners, with more coming from the civil service and transport companies. The age of conscription was to be raised to fifty, and fifty-five in special cases, but men between the ages of forty-two and fifty would not necessarily be sent into the firing lines, they would be used to release younger men from service units and home defence. Although short of men the army had plenty of shells and the reduction in output from Gretna meant that girls were being dismissed and sent home allowing the hostels in Carlisle to be returned to their previous uses or, as in the case of the Central Hotel, equipped as a temporary military hospital.

The first week of the meat rationing scheme 'going live' seemed to go well. Although some of the butchers who served the hotels had meat left because the demand from hotels was reduced, much of this was taken up by others. Butchers had been told that if supplies to them were reduced they had to limit the amounts they gave out to ensure that each household received a similar proportion. There were problems over the use of offal as people were reluctant to exchange their coupons for what they looked on as waste. Hotels too found customers reluctant to part with coupons in return for an indeterminate amount of meat and the demand for fish grew rapidly, to the extent that at the Gretna Tavern virtually no meat meals appeared on the menu. There were problems for soldiers passing through the city and travellers who did not have coupons had to make do with non-meat dishes.

To take the place of the farm workers who had joined up the Board of Agriculture was better prepared with replacements than in previous years. It announced that there would be 60,000 soldiers available in addition to 260,000 women workers, and it was hoped that this figure would rise to 300,000.

One initiative set up to help young people was the Crosby Home Farm School which catered for pupils between the ages of nine and fourteen. The focus was on agriculture and each pupil became a 'bailiff' for part of the farm, responsible for keeping livestock and growing crops to sell on the market. They were also taught a general school curriculum and Vernon Stokes, a well known local artist of mainly animal pictures, took classes in art.

The Education Committee was keen to develop facilities which were not available when Cumberland County Council was responsible. Mr Chance contributed money to establish a science laboratory in memory of his son at Tullie House which would be used by apprentices and others from local firms, particularly those involved in dyeing, engineering, agriculture and for the training of teachers. Opportunities would be given for research, supported by a qualified assistant and a technician, to support local businesses developing new techniques and materials. A number of local companies, including Carr's, Morton Sundour and Hudson Scotts had joined together to provide a guaranteed £1,000 a year for staff costs.

The military representative was still lodging appeals against some exemptions, but the tribunal took the view that as most of the men would be called up under the new regulations there was little point in considering these. Under the regulation any man not graded as 1, fully fit, could apply to remain in his current job, but it had to be a personal application, not from an employer. The Town Clerk was critical of the process when the tribunal on 18 April considered cases of men from

Morton Sundour. One man was employed in inspecting and passing army blankets, the Town Clerk asked whether the military representative 'was on the side of the army, or of the army getting blankets?' Another man had been rejected when in Huddersfield and under national service had come to Carlisle, replacing two men for the army. If he was taken the tribunal was told, then nobody would be left to do the work of two men, 'is this what is wanted?'

After only a couple of weeks of meat rationing the Food Controller announced that a full rationing scheme, covering meat, sugar, and all fats was to be introduced on 13 July. Extra coupons would be included to allow other items to be added as necessary. At the same time the use of potatoes for anything other than human or animal food was banned and the price of soft fruit was fixed to allow jam makers to be able to plan production.

Although there was censorship of letters from the front and the papers had agreed to limit some of the more graphic descriptions that had been evident earlier in the war, some reports of action during the German advance could have fallen into the category of 'giving comfort to the enemy', or it would have done if they were published while the Germans were still pushing south. One letter from a base hospital, written by Sergeant James Martin of 8 Border, who was a tenor in the Cathedral choir told of events during the attack:

> *'What we have endured during the first 4 days of the offensive was terrible and I can't bear to think of it. We had no food and not even water to drink. We slept in wet trenches when we got the chance, which was very seldom, for we were continually digging in at night and holding the enemy back during the day. To be here is just like heaven after the hell that I have left. I was hoping I might have got to 'Blighty' but there is little chance now. I can tell you the enemy's overwhelming numbers has been the cause of our retirement but I have no doubt that we shall hold him.'*

Many men from Carlisle were involved in the retreat and had been overrun or surrounded and taken prisoner. The League had been supporting 180 PoWs on 1 December 1916 which by 21 March 1918 had increased to 460 and by 17 May increased further to 730, involving

Medical staff were still meeting hospital trains. Ashley Kendall

a cost of £29,200, exactly £80 each day. Reports from returned prisoners and others described the poor health of those men from countries which did not send food parcels, they were barely able to survive and if they were made to work they weakened rapidly.

A civic event was held at the Town Hall on 1 May when the Lord Lieutenant, Lord Lonsdale, presented the Order of the British Empire for various acts of bravery to Gretna workers: Miss Norah Morphet of Millholme Avenue, Mrs Joan Nelson, South View Terrace and Miss Ada Watt who lived in the Police House, Port Carlisle. Accidents were not uncommon and these women had been working among the chemicals used for cordite, although censorship prevented details being given. Dealing with the dangers at Gretna were not always directly rewarded as in the case of 17-year-old Agnes Gardiner whose family lived in Carlisle where her father worked for Morton Sundour. When he appealed for exemption from call-up in 1918 he stated that he had twelve children, two of his sons were in the army and his daughter had lost an arm in an accident at Gretna; his appeal was allowed.

Whitsun Bank Holiday weather was fine, in fact too hot to encourage much walking in the countryside. Cyclists took the opportunity to explore the district but those wishing to travel by train to Wetheral and Talking Tarn had to be there early as the first train filled up quickly and the seats on the second had to be booked, and was soon filled. The children's fair on the Sauceries was well attended by a crowd estimated as between 15,000 and 20,000 with much dancing, games playing and general happiness for citizens of all ages. The fine weather also helped to boost the collection on behalf of the Citizens' League PoW fund which raised £464 in the street collection, the largest amount achieved in a day.

Work was underway to address the problems of the tram service. The employment of female drivers allowed the company to release the track men who had been forced to take up driving and resume road maintenance. Work on the track was to be continued over the summer, and four cars had been certificated as being suitable for the use of female drivers.

The demand for men was putting pressure on the agricultural communities. The army had been told it could take a total of 30,000 Grade 1 men from agriculture, starting with those below the age of twenty-five. The local War Agriculture Committee had to consider each case and either agree or disagree that the man was essential to the farm. The feeling was that the total would not be reached by calling up the younger men and so the next group, up to the age of thirty-one, would be involved. Women workers to replace men were still unpopular with farmers. 'Agricola' who wrote in the *Journal* on farming matters commented that women from the Land Army were to be trained by the farmer using land adjoining his 'and I hope he has more success than I did'.

The Whitsun Hirings were very quiet. Experienced men who had been designated as essential to the farm where they were working did not want to risk falling into the army's net by trying to move for more money. Boys were commanding much higher wages than in previous years and the *Journal* published a table comparing earnings pre-war and in 1918. Men's rates had gone up from a maximum of £20 to £47 for a half year for an experienced man; for the next group, 'good men' it had increased from £13 to £40 and for boys from £9 to £30. Girls' and women's rates had also gone up, from £14 to £24 for women and £8 to £12 for girls. These rates were well in excess of those set by the Agricultural Wages Board from southern counties showing how the shortage of skilled labour in the north affected the market. The changes

Adverts aimed at women increased as the war went on. Cumbrian Newspapers Ltd

and regulations brought in during the war were reportedly encouraging older farmers to think of retiring while they still had money available. This allowed new men to come into the business and encouraged sons to take on the family farms earlier than might have been the case.

The meat ration was increased in mid-May, because more supplies of frozen meat were arriving in the country. Farmers had been asked to keep immature animals for fattening, as it was feared that to use the fattening stock would result in the country being totally dependent on imported meat. Farmers were more willing to engage 20,000 schoolboys to help with the harvest than to work with female labour. The Minister of National Service requested schools to release boys to attend camps which had proved successful in the previous two years. The boys would be paid 4d an hour and the government gave 5s weekly allowance for food. The period for their engagement was lengthened which meant some would miss schooling described as 'a sacrifice which war demands of a nation'.

The Volunteers were placed in a dilemma by a request from the War

Office for them to offer their services for up to three months of garrison duty to relieve regulars who could be sent to France. The problem they faced was that most of those who remained after the last call-up were there because they had been exempted by tribunals on the grounds that they were carrying out work of national importance. To offer to leave this for three months was thought to show that perhaps what they were doing was not so vital and the army might try to have certificates revoked. Most of the men would have preferred to be called up to carry out the duty but the War Office wanted to deal with volunteers.

Major Edward Chance was killed on 29 May leading a battalion of the Leicestershire Regiment. A Regular officer, he had been in the war from the beginning and wounded in September 1914. It was the second son lost to Frederick Chance and his wife Mary who had done so much for the civilian war effort in the city.

One of the attempts to improve child health, the provision of playgrounds, was also the responsibility of the Health Committee which was asking for suggestions of suitable locations from their critics who were complaining at the lack of provision in some parts of the city. One idea, to make use of school playgrounds was to be considered by the Education Committee but one council member pointed out that since most of the schools were in heavily populated districts the use of the playgrounds would disturb the sleep of night working rail men and other shift workers.

The city press identified a major social change when the Mayor, Bertram Carr, failed to get a seconder to his motion of protest against the Health Committee's agreement of allowing a Sunday concert in Bitts Park on 16 June. His argument was that although the request was based on charity 'there was something repugnant and distasteful in doing anything which might encourage the secularisation of the Sabbath'. The *Journal* leader described the lack of public sympathy for this view as being based on the success of the regular Sunday concerts being held in London and other major cities which were thought to be consistent to the 'style of the day'.

The conflicting demands of providing food and getting men into the army were tested at the military tribunal on 14 June when the chairman refused to allow the army to take a baker for the South End Co-op who was one of the men making 25,000 loaves a week; he was exempted. A butcher who was single-handedly running a business with over 2,000 registered customers was also given exemption. Sausage making on a commercial scale, over 10,000lbs a week, was threatened when the military appealed against John Rogers who worked for Cavaghan and Gray; he too was exempted.

The introduction of butter control in mid-June led to a huge outcry. Butter was used by many families as a substitute for meat, and in the summer many families' main meal was potatoes with butter. The weekly allowance of 5oz per person was hopelessly inadequate and a meeting of food committees from the north recommended a postponement of the scheme until the end of September. The rationing of amounts faced the producers with a forced reduction in the amount they could sell, few could find alternative markets as they sold direct to the public in open markets, to allow the wholesalers to get hold of the supply would lead to them keeping control once the war was over. Farmers had the cows already producing the milk from which they churned the butter, and this supply could not be suddenly cut off.

Although there is no evidence of the 'white feather' campaigns reported in some cities the taking of men aged over forty-one caused some women to get the names and addresses of younger men not in the army and pursue them to find out why. The military authorities defended these men by saying that in their view there were no younger men who did not have a certificate of some sort exempting them from service. A raid on a billiard hall in Carlisle netted 135 men, all holding a certificate of one sort or another.

A meeting of the temperance movement in Carlisle on 20 June agreed to ask the Mayor to set up a public meeting on prohibition in the city. Speakers gave credit to the Control Board for taking the process part of the way but thought that if Carlisle gave the lead other parts of the country would follow. Referendums were planned in many cities but the stance taken by Carlisle would, it was thought, be critical.

The *Journal* on 21 June reported an outbreak of what was being called Spanish influenza or Flanders fever. Sufferers of the symptoms, mild fever, headache and sickness were advised to go to bed for the short period that the illness seemed to be taking to clear. There had been a larger outbreak in Lancashire with just a few cases in Carlisle but it was said to be very infectious in its early stages. The paper said that although there had been cases of flu there had been no great

Italian Royal Carabinieri Band at the Gretna Tavern. Ashley Kendall

outbreak in the previous twenty years.

By 28 June the outbreak had spread. The symptoms were still quite mild but quick in becoming established, described as 'a sniff, a sneeze, a shiver and a faint'. Attendance at some schools fell rapidly as did the number of workers in some businesses as the virus spread through the workplaces. One Carlisle chemist put forward the theory that the cause was not the transfer of germs but the constant bombardments in France which released hydrogen and carbon. He advised the use of carbide of lime to release oxygen as the best way to combat the spread.

The virus took hold in the following week when the number of workers infected rose sharply. One third of the staff at Tyers were off sick, 400 were absent from Carr's and 60 from Pratchitt's the shell factory; school absence returns showed rates between thirty per cent and seventy-three per cent. The first death was that of 15-year-old Walter Wardrop, an employee of Carr's who died on 27 June.

The 2 July issue of the *Journal* contained the announcement of the award of eleven Victoria Crosses, one of them to a man who was born in Jarrow but moved with his family to Carlisle. Second Lieutenant Joseph Henry Collin, of the King's (Royal Lancaster) Regiment, was fatally wounded on 9 April, two days before his twenty-fifth birthday, when the post he was defending with five other men was overwhelmed by the German advance. In the middle of July Miss Toupie Lowther was awarded the Croix de Guerre for her work in running a fleet of ambulances in support of the French forces.

Hers was the second Croix de Guerre to be awarded to a woman from the district. In 1917 Beauchamp Waddell, the VAD nurse arrested as a spy and then bombed by a Zeppelin in Calais early in the war had transferred to ambulance driving. She was wounded and while in hospital in June 1917 recovering from the amputation of a leg she was presented with the award. Another local woman, Margaret Ellison Duckers, whose parents lived in Wetheral died in Salonica on 16 May. She had nursed in Liverpool before joining the Queen Alexandra Nursing Service. Her brother Scott, who was the centre of a conscientious objector's case earlier in the war was still in prison.

The needs of the war re-energised the salvage scheme which encouraged householders to collect metal, material and other items such as bones which were used to make explosives. The cost of other services was increasing with a proposal to raise the price of gas by 9d per 1,000 cubic feet. This was to cover the £2,000 loss in the previous year and to meet the increased costs of production and labour. Internment charges at the Stanwix, Carlisle and Upperby Cemeteries were increased by fifty per cent. Instructions were issued to the public setting out how they were supposed to complete and use their ration books which were being distributed in time for the scheme to be implemented on 14 July covering the supply of butter, lard, sugar and meat, including cooked meat.

The Mayor was among a group of men whose cases were heard by the military tribunal. His exemption for six months was not opposed by the military representative but other cases were more fiercely debated. Murray Morton of Morton Sundour argued that the men who were being considered were doing a better job for the war effort than if they were forced to take on unskilled jobs in the army. He was supported by the Town Clerk who gave examples of men who had been senior clerks in his department who were now doing basic clerical work for the army. Mr Morton cited two cases of council clerks, one now driving a mule team and the other cleaning out horses, neither of them skilled jobs.

Changes and concern over rationing continued throughout July. The value of the meat coupons was reduced but ham and bacon were removed from the ration, at least temporarily.

Fuel rationing featured in the papers on 6 August; householders were going to have to apply for their allocations of coal, coke, electricity and gas based on the size of the house and their consumption in the previous year. Coal stocks declined across the country, partly because of the number of miners called to the army and not replaced. One suggestion that German prisoners could be used to work underground was rejected as unsafe by the Miners' Union; using women to carry out surface work was also rejected. The supplies from France and Belgium were non-existent and the carriage of coal for the use of troops in France was a critical supply. The miners were, the owners claimed, working just three or four days in each week, and strikes were still happening. The obvious alternative fuel, wood, was in relatively good supply in Cumberland, even the trimmings from the trees felled by the Canadians would give a reasonable stock for the city, but transporting was relatively expensive and landowners were unwilling to let people onto their land to forage for fallen timber. Later in August it was still the means of lighting fires rather than the fuel that was in short supply. The stock of matches in shops in the city ran out and people had to find ways to light fires, cookers and for some, more importantly, cigarettes and pipes. Eventually in early October after many attempts to iron out problems the coal and power rationing scheme was postponed.

Carlisle received visitors from Australia, New Zealand and South Africa; these followed others from Canada and the United States. All were journalists on tours of Britain organised by the Ministry of Information. They were shown the work of the Control Board and the taverns and inns in the city. Gretna was a source of amazement to all the groups, particularly the fact that it had been a green field site in 1915. They were also impressed by the quality of the housing and social facilities provided, and the support given by the welfare women to the girls from all over the north who had arrived to stay in the hostels.

Criticism of the national government grew: it was being seen as losing energy and drive. The cost of maintaining certain departments was questioned, not least the War Office which was thought to be the resting place of many officers who could be better employed at the front. Generally there was a feeling as the war seemed to be progressing better, that some members of the government and civil service may have been allowed to get away with wasting money and keeping themselves comfortable.

A cold autumn led many people to ignore advice about saving coal for later in the year. A case was put forward that supported a greater allowance for the county, particularly because much of the locally produced coal was being sent to other towns and cities. Stocks of coal continued to fall throughout the autumn as production fell by 13million tons, a consequence of the removal of 75,000 more men from the mines.

The Food Controller attempted to make the supply of fresh and frozen meat equable across the country. Locally people argued that they were not used to eating frozen meat. The cost of transporting fresh meat from the area and having to pay to carry in the replacement frozen meat was seen to be a waste of coal and unnecessary pressure on transport.

The work of the Citizens' League was again praised when the Central Prisoners of War Committee described the Carlisle scheme as one of the most efficient in the country. The committee said it had no problems with the Border Regiment as the League was so efficient at keeping records and providing the necessary parcels. They had to find £672 per week to provide the 872 parcels for the Border men in Germany. The League had also collected £82,000 for the war effort. The total turnover of the League for 1917 amounted to £118,860, an increase of £100,000 on the previous year, caused by the regular use of the Rest Room and the huge increase in the number of PoW parcels.

The *Journal* on 8 October had a series of headlines 'THE GERMAN RETREAT; RETIREMENT NEAR CAMBRAI; DOUAI IN FLAMES; FRENCH ADVANCE IN CHAMPAGNE; RHEIMS SET FREE; GERMAN PEACE OVERTURES'. The only question being would the Germans ask for terms before the Allies crossed the border? By the following weeks the headlines read 'GREAT BRITISH VICTORY; CAMBRAI IN RUINS; 11,000 PRISONERS AND 200 GUNS TAKEN; HASTY GERMAN RETREAT; ALLIES CLOSE TO LE CATEAU'.

The visitors to the city on 12 October were rather more colourful

Italian Royal Carabinieri Band turning into Bank Street from Lowther Street.
Ashley Kendall

Italian Royal Carabinieri Band in English Street. Ashley Kendall

than the gentlemen of the press who had been seen in September. The Italian Carabinieri Band complete with instruments and ornate uniforms were in the city to demonstrate appreciation of the co-operation between Britain and Italy and to collect money for the Red Cross. The band had been in Britain for about four weeks and their visit to Carlisle was part of the tour. Met by the Mayor, the band paraded through the streets which were lined with a cheering crowd as they made their way to lunch at the Gretna Tavern. After speeches and toasts the band played in the Market Place to a large crowd in the fine weather. The Border Regiment band marched with the Carabinieri and led them back to the station where, at 4pm, they boarded a train for Blackpool.

Food regulations proliferated during October limiting the amount of jam and marmalade available; children aged below 18 were allowed an additional ration. The proportion of potato in bread was increased as soon as the main crop became available. Butter supplies fluctuated week to week. Some farmers who had insufficient stocks gave back coupons to registered customers. This caused frustration and anger as simply handing back coupons did not help the housewife who was

Making wheat go further by using potatoes. A change from 1917 when it was the potato in short supply. Cumbrian Newspapers Ltd

How to use Potatoes in making Bread.

THE following is a recipe for home bread making: *Ingredients*—7 lbs. flour, 1½ oz. salt, 2 oz. Calders Yeast, 3½ lbs. water, ½ lb. potatoes.

Wash the potatoes and boil in their skins. When cooked, strain, peel and mash. Then weigh ½ lb. potatoes and 7 lbs. flour. Put the flour, salt and potatoes into a basin and mix well. Heat up to 82 degrees. Dissolve the Calders Yeast in the 3½ lbs. water, which should be maintained at a temperature of 90 degrees. Add the yeast to the other ingredients. Mix well and knead for 10 minutes. Place on a table free from draught for 1½ hours, then knead again and cover up for one hour more. Next divide the mixture, mould into the shapes required and place in slightly warmed and greased tins. Allow it to rise for 30 minutes before placing it in the oven.

Bake at a temperature of 420 degrees. Loaves 1 lb. weight bake in half an hour. 2 lb. loaves will take 50 minutes. As experience is gained it will be found that the quantity of potatoes can be increased from ½ lb. to 1 lb.

Calders Yeast, made from the Barley of Bonnie Scotland is delightfully fresh.

Local Distributing Depot: Lowthians Lane, Carlisle. Also at Maryport, Workington, Keswick, Kendal, Barrow and Ulverston.

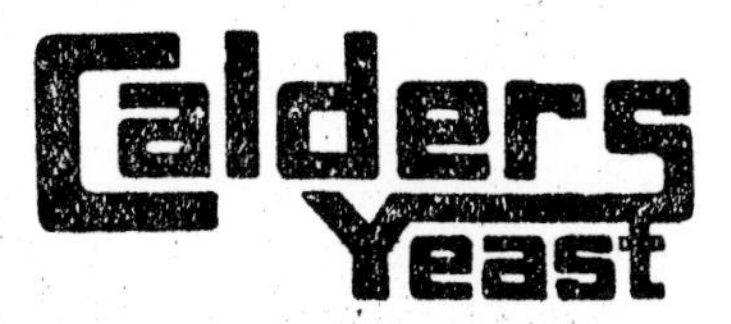

CALDERS YEAST COMPANY, LIMITED, Calder House, Newcastle-on-Tyne.

generally unable to find a shop with spare stocks of margarine, let alone butter.

Recreational activities continued to appear in the press reports. A meeting of the Border Coursing Association attracted more dogs and their owners to chase hares near Longtown. The first meeting of the Carlisle and District Cage Bird Society was held on 12 October. These enthusiasts had been keeping their birds all during the conflict despite the cost of feed.

As with other regulations failure to comply with the complicated rules about ration books resulted in people ending up before the magistrates on 11 October. Most blatant was the case of Mary Atkinson who had sold a rabbit without taking a coupon, telling the purchaser that if they were caught she knew they would be in trouble. She was fined a huge £2 as a deterrent to others.

On the afternoon of the same day 37-year-old Tamar Noble was accused of fraudulently attempting to get another ration book in the name of her husband who was living in Hawick and had his own book. She claimed that her husband was just working away and she expected him to return as she was used to him being away for some months. It wasn't a good day for Tamar as in the court that same morning she had failed in her case to get her husband to pay maintenance on the grounds that he was living with another woman in Hawick. He gave evidence against her in the ration book case saying that he had not been home for ten months. In something of a tangled web, she was fined £2.

Canon Rawnsley used the occasion of the annual doctors' and nurses' service in the cathedral to reflect on what Carlisle had contributed to the care of wounded soldiers in 1918. The 560 beds at Fusehill and the associated VAD hospitals had looked after 7,963 patients; the other VAD hospitals had cared for 1,118 soldiers. The system of getting men from the station to the hospitals was more secure than earlier in the war as there were eleven ambulances and six lorries which met the ambulance trains as they arrived at the station and transferred the men.

Recruiting of women continued to the Land Army and the Queen Mary Auxiliary Army Corps. A meeting in Carlisle on 19 October was told that 30,000 women were needed to join the Corps to help the British Army and 15,000 more to help the Americans. Their role would be to undertake tasks behind the lines to release men for the front. From a small start the Corps had grown to 50,000 serving with the forces, mainly as cooks, but others were working as clerks; tailors, mending and patching uniforms; bakers and munitions workers.

The flu epidemic in Carlisle during the summer appeared to have died out by November with very few cases and only one death recorded, but Brampton was suffering from a more severe outbreak. Cases in Carlisle were mainly linked to the return of soldiers from France and the Medical Officer put up posters showing how to avoid the spread of the virus. Manufacturers were not slow in tying their products to the outbreak; Oxo advertised its benefits in helping to combat the virus by 'fortifying the system'.

A service of remembrance for the men killed in the conflict was held in the cathedral on 3 November. The Mayor, with his mace and sword bearer together with the Town Clerk and members of the council, attended as did officers from the Castle and ministers of other churches. A rumour circulated throughout the country on 7 November that an Armistice had been signed, but the delight was short lived.

Hermione Lediard, daughter of Dr Henry Lediard and his wife was another civilian casualty of the war. She had arranged and played in concerts for the Lonsdale Battalion and other events in the early years. She was a member of the VAD who worked at the Chadwick Memorial Hospital. In 1916 at the age of twenty-four she went to train as a nurse at Oxford where she contracted blood poisoning which, in the days before penicillin, was often fatal. She was returned home where, after being ill for about a month, she died.

The Armistice was signed on 11 November. The *Journal* of 12 November described the scenes in the city during the previous twenty-four hours. The paper had posted an announcement of the armistice that morning on a notice board which attracted a large crowd outside the offices in English Street. The cheering of the group attracted others, some carrying flags, and more people, including wounded soldiers, arrived in the Market Square. A telephone call from the paper's office to the Mayor in his office at Carr's resulted in the factory's hooter being sounded, soon afterwards joined by the siren at Buck's. These two were the signal for all the other sirens and bells in the city to be sounded and rung, including the anti-Zeppelin buzzer on the gas works. At the Drill Hall the Union Flag was raised and the workers joined in singing patriotic songs until they were dismissed for the day. Other businesses

Bertram Carr announcing the Armistice. Ashley Kendall

closed, shops put up their shutters and school children were released to join the celebrations.

A few minutes before 11 o'clock the Dean accompanied by Canon and Mrs Rawnsley, Mr Waldron and the boys of the choir, ascended the steps to the top of the Cathedral tower where at 11am the Naval Ensign was unfurled and the choir sang 'God Save the King' and gave three hearty cheers.

Business at the weekly police court in the Town Hall was suspended as the news reached the magistrates and the cheering and sirens indicated what was occurring. The Mayor made his way from Carr's and Canon Rawnsley descended the Cathedral tower steps and the two men, accompanied by the Dean and other prominent citizens, gathered on the Town Hall steps in front of a growing crowd. The Mayor gave a short speech celebrating the end of the war and extolling the work done by the servicemen. He also remembered those who had died in the conflict and the sorrow this had brought to many homes.

The celebrations continued during the morning with wounded

soldiers at the forefront of many impromptu celebrations. Cameras, which had been banned during the war, reappeared and photographs were taken of the crowds and a film made of the celebration.

The sadness of some was typified by a man in tears outside the Town Hall who apologised to those round him saying, 'I cannot rejoice, I have lost three sons'. A little boy in one of the schools burst into tears when his classmates cheered. He just said 'my father will not come home again'.

For the majority the relief at the end of the conflict outweighed at least temporarily personal grief and flags quickly appeared on every building. At the Castle a message received during the night led the officers to believe that it had been signed at 2.30am, so they held an Armistice parade at 9am. Bands played at The Cross all afternoon.

The soldiers in the local hospitals were not slow in joining in the celebrations. Some men from Fusehill drove round the streets in a flag bedecked staff car, returning later with some of the more seriously wounded as passengers. Patients at Murrell Hill were granted a late

Jubilant crowds outside the Town Hall. Ashley Kendall

pass and the staff and patients at the Chadwick were invited to a celebration by Mrs Robinson and her daughter at Eden Bridge Hospital. The evening included what was described as a 'sumptuous feast' with entertainment and a whist drive.

The focus of celebration moved to the Castle in the evening where the soldiers had completed an effigy of the Kaiser and doused their bonfire in oil. As the crowd gathered at 8.30pm the regimental band struck up and marched around the square playing *John Peel.* When they had completed one circuit the bonfire was lit and the effigy consumed in the flames. The band continued to play until it fell when they changed the tune to *Rule Britannia* and the crowd joined in singing and then with the three cheers given 'to our boys at the front'. The glow of the fire attracted more to the Castle and by the end of the evening there were several thousand people singing along with the band in a selection of popular songs and cheering the national anthems of the Allies as they were played. Celebrations ended about 9.30pm and the darkened streets were once again crowded with people singing as they went home.

Action to dismantle the machinery of war began swiftly. Notices of conscription and call-up for medical examination were cancelled as were any outstanding tribunal cases. By 22 November the Ministry of Munitions had published an order giving the sequence of discharge of the remaining munitions workers.

The General Election Campaign began on Saturday 16 November. Theodore Carr was adopted by the Liberal and Conservative Alliance on the same afternoon and the local Labour Party had already selected Ernest Lowthian as its candidate. Richard Denman announced his decision not to stand for re-election, supporting the candidature of Theodore Carr for the Alliance.

Bertram Carr, in his speech accepting a second term as Mayor, set out an agenda for improvement of the city. He listed the need for a new public hall; the resolution of the financial adjustment between county and city which had been running since 1914; the gas works needed urgent rebuilding; the tramway had improved as a result of prompting by the council but had to be maintained; the opening of the science laboratory funded by Mr Chance would, it was hoped, form the basis of a technical institute.

CHAPTER 8

Afterword, 1919 and Beyond

Troops return – Celebrations – Creating a memorial – Control Board remains – Gretna closed

It took until 1920 for all the troops, particularly those who had been conscripted, to return. The last back were the Territorials of 4 Border who had spent the war in India and Burma. Civilians like Mr Molyneux, interned in Germany since 1914, also made their way back

Rydal Street Party 1919. Ashley Kendall

Peace party, possibly St Nicholas Street 1919. Ashley Kendall

Peace Dinner, Carlisle Market, September 1919. Ashley Kendall

to the city. Soldiers who had been badly wounded were released from hospital. Movement was not all one way and the farewell tea for fifty remaining Belgian refugees was held at the beginning of January 1919. Other celebrations were held in July and September when many communities got together to celebrate in street parties.

The Citizens' League had to consider what to do with the funds it had accumulated. The decision was taken in 1920 to buy Rickerby Park for £11,500 and, with support from the council, erect a war memorial there and build another link to the city by opening a memorial footbridge. The park remains as public open space. Many of the 'old stagers' on the city council decided they had done their bit and stood aside to let younger men, many who had been in the Citizens' League, take over. Theodore Carr won the 1918 election and served one term as an MP; he was in third place in the 1922 election which was won by George Middleton.

Families of all classes had to get used to peace. Many women finished working, but some remained in employment. Men returned to take up the jobs which had been kept open for them. Many did not return and widows received pensions. Transport, roads, trains and trams

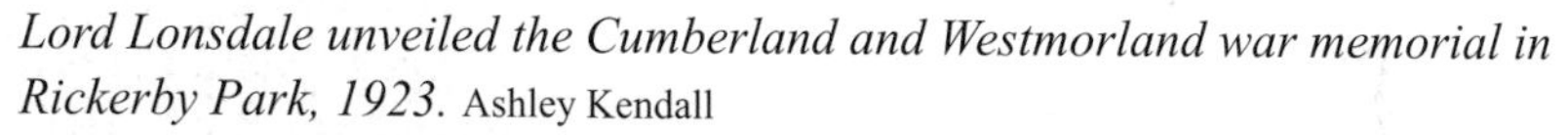

Lord Lonsdale unveiled the Cumberland and Westmorland war memorial in Rickerby Park, 1923. Ashley Kendall

Memorial Bridge to Rickerby Park, paid for by the Citizens' League. John Hughes

had to be refurbished and repaired. Hotels used as hostels were returned to their peacetime role.

The longest lasting change was that of the Control Board which remained in operation until 1971. The cause of the control, the munition works at Gretna, was much more quickly removed from the landscape. By 1919 many of the workers had returned home and in 1921 the sale of the equipment and machinery was advertised. This sale took place in 1922 resulting in the demolition of many of the buildings and the materials being sold for scrap; this was followed two years later by the sale in Carlisle of the housing and other accommodation on the site.

Rickerby Park had played many roles in the war, home to Belgian Refugees and Canadian Foresters. Denis Perriam

The city resumed its role as a transport hub, particularly involved in the restoration of railway services. Banks and services remained in business and, as in other places, went through amalgamations and other changes.

There is little doubt that the city did achieve what Denman described in his 1917 speech by becoming a city that learned to work as a community. People of all classes contributed what they could to defeating Germany. The Citizens' League and its members were probably the pinnacle of achievement by providing leadership without looking for individual reward. They had a flexible approach to solving myriad problems and being very effective at what would now be called networking. The city had much to be proud of; the citizens had been tested, not by shell and bomb, but by huge and tumultuous social change at a time when nearly half of the settled population were not at home and the future was anything but clear.

Bibliography

Brader, C. A world on wings; young female workers and cinema in World War 1, *Women's History Review* Vol 14 No 1 2005

Carlisle Journal 1914 - 1919

Cumberland News 1914 - 1919

Emmett, C. and Templeton, J. *Carlisle Through Time*, Amberley Publishing 2010

Richards, J. and Searle, A. *The Quintinshill Conspiracy*, Pen and Sword 2013

Routledge, G.L. *Gretna's Secret War*, Bookcase, Carlisle 1999

Scott-Parker, M. *Carlisle Grammar School*, Parker-Leigh Publishing 2008

Seabury, O. *The Carlisle State Management Scheme*, Bookcase, Carlisle 2007

Perriam, D. and Ramshaw, D. *Carlisle Citadel Station*, P3 Publications, Carlisle 1998

Websites:

http://www.donmouth.co.uk/ Munitionettes football match reports and pictures

www.devilsporridge.co.uk/Devils Porridge Museum, Daleside, Butterdales, Eastriggs, Annan, Dumfriesshire DG12 6TQ

Index